GET DISMISSED: THE SEQUEL

JUST WHEN YOU THOUGHT IT WAS SAFE TO DRIVE IN CALIFORNIA AGAIN.

GET YOUR TRAFFIC TICKET DISMISSED, WITHOUT GOING TO COURT.

STEVEN F. MILLER
&
ALEXIS C. VEGA

Lasagna 2018 Sawyer's Office Reference Guide

Revised: February 2018

This book was written to provide information related to issues in California. Every effort has been made to make it as complete and as limited as possible, but no warranty of purposes or fitness is implied. All information is provided on an "as is" basis and is offered as information only. The author and publisher shall have any liability to any person or entity with respect to any loss or damage caused or alleged to be caused directly or indirectly arising from the information contained in this book.

Published By:

GoCGLicense.com
1770 Certa Ave, Suite 196 West Los Angeles CA

ISBN: 13 978 0692997307
SAN: 19 0692 9973 xx

Contents

Introduction

Let's get right to the point here: Why do you need this book? Answer: TIME and MONEY! Read on and that statement will make total sense.

There is a better way to fight traffic tickets in California...and we know what it is! That's what the brain trust here at GetDismissed has been evangelizing about for the past 14 years, while helping tens of thousands of drivers successfully fight their traffic tickets.

So, what is this "better way," and what exactly can be done when you receive a traffic ticket? Should you just pay the ticket? Go to traffic school? No, there are better options available. Should you go to court and fight the ticket yourself? Hire an expensive attorney to fight the ticket for you? Those methods could waste even more time and money than your first options. We have better ideas, and we will share them with you in this book.

Why should you read this book instead of others? There are many books that deal with traffic tickets and how to fight them, but this is the ONLY book that gives you the best roadmap of options on how to fight your ticket.

GET DISMISSED: THE SEQUEL

Have you ever been to traffic court? Not a fun experience. Typically, it is you and about a hundred other people who are also not thrilled to be spending the day in traffic court. Once everyone is present, the bailiff stands up and announces he can "do you a favor" and grant traffic school immediately, for those who are eligible. If you don't accept traffic school, the bailiff will follow up by telling you not to fight your ticket because they will NOT grant you traffic school if you fight the ticket and lose. The bailiff then makes a final, simple, announcement: YOU WILL LOSE.

As a result, approximately 75 percent of the people in that jam-packed courtroom simply accept traffic school and gratefully run for the doors. Why do the courts do this? Simple. It all comes back to TIME and MONEY. When a person stays in the courtroom and takes up the court's time by fighting their ticket (whether they win or lose), that person is costing the court more time and money than the fine they can collect for the traffic ticket. The whole thing becomes a matter of simple economics, the court's time is more valuable than the fine from your ticket. Probably a LOT more.

Wouldn't it be great if there were a system that provided drivers all the exact same rights under the law to contest a traffic ticket, but also didn't waste the court's precious time and money? Well, we have good news for you. There is such a system, and it's called a "Trial by Written Declaration."

Trial by Written Declarations have been around since 1978 and provides unlucky or unfortunate drivers with a very quick, very simple, and very effective solution for fighting traffic tickets. The Trial by Written Declaration process can be found on the back of every single traffic ticket issued and gives drivers an option to contest their traffic ticket in writing without ever having to step foot in a courtroom.

Drivers complete the documents and submit them to the court by mail instead of going into court to contest the traffic ticket in person. This "by mail" option - the Trial by Written Declaration - is the best way to contest a traffic ticket in California and eliminates the need for you to waste your time fighting your ticket in court.

Before we move on, we would like to make a bold prediction right here, right now. In the not-so-distant future, the day will come when you will not even be able to go to court to contest your traffic ticket in California. In fact, in California there is an effort to move traffic tickets from the criminal court system into the civil court system. This would also end the current criminal court's rules that require the evidence to show guilt beyond a reasonable doubt and instead reduce the burden of proof to show that the driver more likely than not committed the traffic infraction. We believe that this prediction will come true within the next 10 years. Why do we believe this? Our prediction is centered on two fundamental principles: TIME and MONEY.

Now back to our prediction: The Trial by Written Declaration process is the only way for the court to save time and money and will take contesting traffic tickets out of the courts due to simple necessity. This will be done to reduce costs while still ensuring the taxpayer's rights. There is no other way. Period.

The GetDismissed service facilitates the process for completing and filing a Trial by Written Declaration with the court. Simply take a picture of your traffic ticket and another picture of your driver license, answer a few questions, download the documents and "voila," your Trial by Declaration is completed for you and ready for you to file with the court.

Like we said earlier, this is why you need this book and why you need GetDismissed; together, they will save you TIME and MONEY.

About The GetDismissed Service:

The GetDismissed Service helps you prepare all the Trial by Written Declaration documents necessary to submit to the court to fight your traffic ticket.

"It works too well. I'd like to arrest the guy who invented this thing."
–Ron Souther CHP Officer (retired)

What is GetDismissed? Well, have you ever wanted to fight a California traffic ticket but didn't know what to do or didn't want to go to court to do it? Well that's what GetDismissed (www.GetDismissed.com) is all about.

GetDismissed is an easy to use web service and mobile application that allows California drivers to simply fight a traffic ticket without going to court. For over 14 years, the brain trust behind GetDismissed has assisted tens of thousands of California drivers with contesting their traffic tickets. Even if you don't currently have a traffic ticket, the GetDismissed service is for you. We provide California drivers, the ability to protect their driving record with a GetDismissed annual membership and fight California traffic tickets for FREE.

GET DISMISSED: THE SEQUEL

Why is this app important? Up until recently the only options available for fighting traffic tickets were to go to court yourself or hire an expensive attorney to contest your traffic ticket for you. And you just know how those options would usually turn out. Then, services like www.ticketbust.com were developed to facilitate the process of completing and filing a Trial by Written Declaration so you didn't have to go to court. Those online services charge fees that are significantly less than what an attorney would charge but still cost a few hundred big ones. Now, thanks to the GetDismissed App, there is a cheaper, more efficient option.

Did you know that there are over 4 million traffic infractions issued for tickets every year in California? Only seven percent of those tickets are ever contested. That is unbelievable! This means that 93% of all tickets issued in California NEVER GET CONTESTED. A truly shocking figure that led us to ask some important questions: Is it too costly for the average person to contest a traffic ticket? Does it take too much time? Is contesting a traffic ticket just too confusing and time consuming? Or are people so absolutely frustrated with the process, or the fact that they received a traffic ticket in the first place, to even try to deal with it. The answer turned out to be an emphatic "YES!" to all those questions. And that is where we come in.

The team at GetDismissed.com have been contesting traffic tickets for decades and started thinking about how technology can be applied to this problem in order to find a more efficient solution. We realized that most people have a mobile phone and most mobile phones have cameras. We also know that it is becoming very common for banking institutions to accept photos of checks for deposit into a person's account. From there it was only natural for us to develop a way to use a cell phone camera to take a picture of a traffic ticket that can then be used in creating a Trial by Written Declaration.

With our team of attorneys, engineers, and designers, along with our marketing agency, we looked for a way to simplify the ticket fighting process in California in order to remove the frustration associated with fighting a ticket in court. Our goal was to create an easy to use system that alleviates that frustration. At the same time, we wanted to offer the most cost-effective way to contest and dismiss a traffic ticket ever seen in the state of California.

We are very proud to say that all of those goals have been achieved and realized with the GetDismissed service. GetDismissed provides California drivers a solution that revolutionizes the traffic ticket fighting process. Now there is NO reason not to contest your traffic ticket. It is no longer "too costly," or "too much work" to do. Even better, if your traffic ticket gets dismissed you will not get any points on your driving record or pay any fines. It will be as if you never received the ticket in the first place. And, one of the best features of a Trial by Written Declaration is that even if your ticket doesn't get dismissed, you've lost almost nothing. You'll be right back where you started, meaning that you can still go to court or take traffic school, if eligible. There's "no harm, no foul," and therefore no reason not to try GetDismissed. Keep reading to find out exactly why and how this whole process works. So now that you have all this information, we predict that you won't want to drive without having a GetDismissed membership.

Of course, we are not suggesting you run out and try to get a traffic ticket so you can use the GetDismissed service. In fact, we offer a membership service to protect you and your driving record. You don't even have to have a traffic ticket to have a GetDismissed membership. And the best part is that you will be able to fight your traffic tickets for FREE. It's also perfectly fine if you want to wait until you receive your next ticket since statistics show that you will probably get another ticket within the next 18 months.

Go ahead and download the app or add a GetDismissed membership. Then, just sit back and wait for that next traffic ticket with confidence because you are now prepared to fight it with GetDismissed.

About The Authors

Steven F. Miller
CEO/President and Founding Member of
The Ticket Advocate, LLC.

Steve has been leading the fight against traffic tickets for over 14 years, practically inventing this industry. Originally, Steve served as President and Founder of TicketBust.com and is now with GetDismissed.com. Steve formed TicketBust.com in 2004, with one goal in mind; to help drivers contest and dismiss their traffic tickets quickly, easily, and inexpensively. Since then Steve has continued to expand TicketBust.com by developing and deploying all the necessary solutions to assist drivers with contesting their traffic tickets. Steve has been featured as an authority on many television, radio, and online networks discussing traffic tickets in California. In addition to being a thought leader and business entrepreneur, Steve is also a published author.

Based on the knowledge acquired while developing and running a successful traffic ticket service in California, Steve knew that there had to be an easier, simpler, and better way to contest a traffic ticket. Steve set out to create a new and revolutionary way to contest a traffic ticket by enabling the masses of people receiving tickets and empowering them with the ability to fight back. Thus, the GetDismissed service was born and released in February, 2015.

GET DISMISSED: THE SEQUEL

Initially raising development funds from friends and family to release and test market GetDismissed, Steve was subsequently able to complete a round of angel financing at a $3M valuation. Steve has now transformed GetDismissed into a membership service that allows all California drivers to contest their traffic tickets for free.

Steve is a published author, releasing his first book in 2011, "Traffic Tickets. Don't Get Mad. Get Them Dismissed. Traffic Ticket Tips, Must Knows, and Much More", and then followed it up in 2012 with, "Traffic Tickets. Don't Get Mad. Get Them Dismissed. Stories From The Street. The Ones Who GOT OFF".   In 2015, Steve released his third book "GetDismissed: No Brainwork Required, It's That Simple".

Steve has also been featured on TV, Radio, Print, and Online as a traffic ticket expert talking about such subjects as distracted driving, contesting traffic tickets, traffic ticket myths, traffic ticket tips, traffic law, and more.

Prior to TicketBust.com, Steve was CEO of MediaHippo, Inc., an interactive agency focused on web, DVD, and multimedia development. Steve was instrumental in promoting and marketing the Kodak Photo CD technology in the 1990's, authored many articles and was a featured speaker at numerous industry events. Steve graduated from California State University Northridge with a BS in Accounting. Steve worked for Deloitte Haskins and Sells as a Certified Public Accountant, prior to starting his own accounting agency.

GET DISMISSED: THE SEQUEL

Alexis C. Vega
Attorney and Member of The Ticket Advocate, LLC.

Having law enforcement officers for parents, Alexis always had a special interest in Criminal Law, specifically Traffic Law.

After earning her law degree and license to practice, Alexis represented defendants in traffic court, as a solo practitioner, handling cases involving failures to pay or appear, red light camera tickets, speeding tickets, sign violation tickets, and many other types of traffic violations.

Alexis is an original member of The Ticket Advocate and has played an instrumental role in GetDismissed since its inception. Prior to GetDismissed, Alexis served as a member of TicketBust.com's executive management team, leading Legal Research and Development. Alexis continues to help develop new materials and products to help drivers exercise their legal right to contest a traffic violation in California.

In 2010, Alexis graduated from The Colleges of Law, Santa Barbara and Ventura, with the degree of Juris Doctor, and was admitted to the State Bar of California as an attorney and counselor at law in 2013. As an undergraduate, Alexis gained extensive experience while working as an intern at the Superior Court of California, Office of the Public Defender where she assisted with trial preparation, and the California Court of Appeal researching and writing memorandum for the Appellate Justices. Alexis also worked as an intern with the Law Offices of Ronald G. Harrington and Associates assisting with pro bono case files.

Prior to co-authoring her third book, "GetDismissed: No Brainwork Required, It's That Simple", with Steve Miller in 2015, Alexis co-authored: "Traffic Tickets. Don't Get Mad. Get Them Dismissed. Traffic Ticket Tips, Must Knows, and Much More" in 2011, and "Traffic Tickets. Don't Get Mad. Get Them Dismissed. Stories From The Street. The Ones Who GOT OFF" in 2012.

Alexis has been featured as a legal expert on contesting traffic tickets on: PBS SoCal with David Nazar, NBC LA News with Stephanie Elam, and KFWB News 980 Money 101 with Bob McCormick.

Alexis is a member of the State Bar of California and the Ventura County Bar Association. Her pro bono work includes volunteering with California Rural Legal Assistance and San Diego Volunteer Lawyers Program.

Injustices in the California Traffic Ticketing System – No Golden Ticket Here

Maybe you squeaked through an intersection in the first few seconds of a red light, answered your phone instead of letting it go to voicemail, or you just slowed down instead of stopping all the way for a stop sign. As safe as we all try to drive every day, sometimes we make mistakes or bad calls, and as a result, over 4,000,000 traffic tickets are issued every year in California. However, only about seven percent of those tickets are ever contested. What's stopping drivers from fighting their traffic tickets? Is it the promise of convenience and making it "go away" by paying the fine, or is it the lack of understanding and knowledge about all the options you have to handle a traffic ticket? And if you don't pay the fine or appear in court due to financial constraints, you run the very real risk of having your license suspended. There are core injustices and inconveniences in the California traffic ticketing system that can make the process unduly expensive, time-consuming, and unfair for drivers across the state.

Flaws in the traffic ticketing system don't start at the court, but in some cases, on the roads. Police department ticket quotas -- requiring officers to write a minimum amount of tickets in a certain amount of time for traffic infractions -- are against state law, although some California police departments that have imposed unlawful quotas have been exposed in the past few years. In 2013, the LAPD paid a settlement of nearly $6 million in a lawsuit brought by 11 officers in the motorcycle unit who said they were required to write a minimum of 18 traffic tickets each shift. In 2015, a group of six police officers in Whittier (also in Los Angeles County) also filed a suit relating to traffic ticket quotas.

When these quotas are high, so are your chances of being pulled over; it begs the question of what course of action was taken by drivers affected by the traffic ticket quotas in these cities: the unlucky many who were ticketed for minor infractions that may not have been caused by a disregard for safety, but might have been explained by reasonable circumstances. Unfortunately, with these types of injustices in the ticketing system, the taxpayers will ultimately be the ones to pay (literally -- lawsuits are expensive).

If you're going to contest your ticket, you should know that, each traffic ticket that doesn't require a mandatory court appearance can be fought in writing, through a process called a Trial by Written Declaration. This option was implemented in 1978 to lessen the burden on both the court and the driver when contesting a ticket. However, anyone who contests tickets in writing will also need to post "bail," or the amount of the original ticket fine, at the time of contestation. On the other hand, a 2015 Judicial Council action ruled that individuals can contest tickets in person in court without paying the "bail" amount first. Even though the "bail" amount will be returned if you're found "not guilty" and the ticket is dismissed, is this detail what's keeping drivers from contesting in the first place? These separate bail-posting requirements point to an injustice in the court system that imposes a financial burden on those who live far from the court, who can't take a day off work to appear in court, or who don't have the financial ability to post bail. In order to balance this system, there should be no difference between fighting a ticket in court or by mail with a written declaration.

However, the reality is that traffic tickets in California are notoriously expensive: the state has a base fine for each traffic infraction and every city or county adds additional fees, varying the total fine in each court across the state. Totaling up penalty assessment fees, court fees, and surcharges can lead to a ticket being over four times more expensive than the original amount of the written ticket. And not everyone is able to pay these exorbitant fees.

On October 25, 2016, a coalition of legal aid organizations including the American Civil Liberties Union of Northern California filed a suit against the California DMV on behalf of low-income California residents who've had their driver's licenses illegally suspended after failing to pay traffic ticket fines without having the opportunity to prove their financial inability to comply, which according to the ACLU is a violation of their "statutory, due process, and equal protection rights." Simply put, there are many drivers in California whose financial situation is not conducive to paying upwards of $300 on a simple moving violation.

GET DISMISSED: THE SEQUEL

In fact, beginning July, 2017, California has agreed to stop suspending licenses for traffic fines. This will mean that Californians will no longer face losing their driver's licenses just because of unpaid traffic fines. Now this doesn't mean that you don't have to pay a traffic ticket you receive, this just means you won't get your license suspended if you don't.

This points to many inequalities in the process; each step in the system exemplifies unjust elements that must be amended in order for the California traffic ticketing structure to be beneficial (or at least non-detrimental) for police departments, cities, and taxpayers alike.

Traffic Court System Summary

Where it all starts: With literally millions and millions of traffic tickets issued in the State of California each year it's no wonder traffic tickets are the number one reason for you to encounter the court system.

"Traffic rules account for most of the contact by average citizens with law enforcement and the courts."
–Judge Edwin Osborne

Your journey through the California traffic court system begins when a police officer decides to make your day by stopping you for a perceived traffic violation.

When you get pulled over the officer will ask you for several items, including:

• driver license

• proof of the vehicle's registration

• proof that the vehicle or the driver is insured

- the officer may ask you to step out of your vehicle (depending on the situation)

There are three types of tickets you might receive during a traffic stop, each with their own penalties and processing location:

- Parking ticket

  - Penalties: fine.

  - Where it's processed: parking ticket agency usually separate from a courthouse.

- Misdemeanor ticket:

  - Penalties: fine, Department of Motor Vehicles (DMV) record point and possible jail time.

  - Where it's processed: criminal division of a courthouse.

- Infraction ticket:

  - Penalties: fine and DMV record point.

  - Where it's processed: courthouse – traffic section of a courthouse.

The (Somewhat) Slanted Judicial Process
If you are reading this book you've probably received a traffic ticket – or anticipate getting one! Since you will be making

your way through the court system, possibly for the first time, let's first review what it's all about.

California has Superior Courts which are also known as trial courts. These are the courts that process traffic tickets. There are trial courts in each of the state's 58 counties. If you get a ticket this is where you will need to go to take care of it. That is, unless you prepare and submit a Trial by Declaration, and using the GetDismissed app will help you do that.

Whether you're a ticket veteran or a ticket virgin, your experience with the traffic court can be frustrating and unpleasant. Add in the recent state budget cuts that have left traffic divisions overworked and understaffed, you have the ingredients for one long, tiring, and overall bad day.

Ticketed drivers often feel they're at an unfair advantage in dealing with and contesting their tickets through these courts and, quite frankly, they're right.

In practice, traffic cases are treated more casually than other criminal cases. Because of this, it often seems as though the court and law enforcement officers are working together. The burden of proof now feels as if it's been unfairly shifted to the defendant (the ticketed driver disputing the ticket) to prove his or her innocence instead of being considered innocent until proven guilty.

There are a few reasons in particular that may be to blame:

GET DISMISSED: THE SEQUEL

First, the California Constitution permits trial courts to appoint officers such as commissioners to perform judicial tasks that are considered "mediocre." Given the casual manner in which traffic cases are handled many courts use traffic commissioners, a Judge Pro-Tem (which is an attorney filling in as a substitute judge), or in rare circumstances, a "real" Judge to handle the court's traffic related caseload. A court commissioner or traffic referee has the authority to decide if you are guilty or not guilty of a traffic ticket and they have the ability to decide your punishment such as monetary fines, community service or traffic school.

Second, there is no right to a jury trial or to a court-appointed attorney for a traffic infraction; although you can hire your own attorney to appear in court for you. A person who pleads not guilty to an infraction (for example speeding, red light, or cell phone tickets) has the right to a trial before a commissioner or traffic referee. In California, there is also the right to a written trial, or Trial by Written Declaration, which we at GetDismissed feel is the best thing out there in traffic ticket defense for reasons we will discuss in detail shortly.

Third, state prosecutors or district attorneys rarely appear in infraction cases due to economic realities. In other words, it's not in the budget to have prosecutors or assistant district attorneys spend their time dealing with low level issues such as mundane traffic matters. On the other side of the fence, attorneys also rarely appear on behalf of the defense of the driver who is disputing their ticket for the simple reason that the cost of an attorney (at $250 per hour or more) would end up costing much more than the actual fees associated with the ticket, which are usually a few hundred dollars.

For these reasons, ticketed drivers who show up in traffic court often feel intimidated and wind up being cajoled into paying the ticket or accepting traffic school; all the while thanking the judge for the privilege of doing so.

If you've never been to traffic court, let us paint the picture:

- Hundreds of angry, frustrated, confused, and frightened drivers with tickets who are missing a day of work;

- Dozens of grumpy court staff;

- And a bailiff whose rehearsed speech will have you - and everyone else - running for the doors, convinced that traffic school is your only option.

Why get bullied in court when you can GetDismissed instead?

Tipping the Scales of Justice in Your Favor
If there's one thing we know at GetDismissed it's that not all tickets are issued equally. Often times a seemingly valid ticket is turned over or dismissed after being contested. This could be due to the officer not having enough evidence to prove guilt (and remember you are innocent until you are proven guilty) or possibly because of a "fatal flaw" on the ticket; like the wrong violation code or other mitigating circumstance.

GET DISMISSED: THE SEQUEL

So, before you beat yourself up about a ticket you received, stop and consider your options to avoid paying the fine, going to traffic school or appearing in traffic court. In later chapters we discuss how to contest your ticket.

You can go to trial in the traditional sense of appearing physically in court before a judge or you can contest your ticket the modern, convenient, and cost-effective way: in writing without going to court; a personal favorite of ours and soon to be your favorite too!

You Have a Traffic Ticket. Now What?

After the shock of receiving a traffic ticket wears off and the huge argument you just got into with your spouse about the traffic ticket is over, it's now time to figure out just what you're going to do about that darn ticket.

First, turn over your traffic ticket and read the back to gather valuable information. On the back of every traffic ticket you will see a list of all your options. The truth is most people are so frustrated at the fact that they even received a traffic ticket that they just throw it in the glove box or on the floor and don't read the information provided to them. All your available options are there for you including:

· **Pay the fine (bail)** – contact the court for bail information. You will not have to appear in court. You will be convicted of the violation and it will appear on your record at the DMV;

· **Appear in court** – Send a certified or registered letter postmarked no later than five days prior to the appearance date or go to the court on the appearance date to request a court trial on a future date when the ticketing officer and any witnesses will be present. But if you do this you will still be required to submit the bail amount;

· **Correct the violation (if applicable)** – If the "Yes" box is checked on the front of your ticket then the violation is correctable. Upon correction of the violation have a law enforcement officer or an authorized inspection/installation station agent sign the back of the ticket. Registration and driver license violations may also be certified as corrected at an office of the DMV or by any clerk of a court in the traffic division. The violation will be dismissed by the court after proof of correction has been submitted and payment of a transaction fee are presented to the court by mail or in person by the appearance date. Violations for auto insurance will be dismissed only upon showing the court evidence of financial responsibility valid at the time of the ticket;

· **Request traffic school (if eligible)** – You may be able to avoid getting a point, a negative mark, on your driving record by completing traffic school. You must pay the ticket amount, a fee to the court for letting you take traffic school, and a fee to the traffic school for the class you take. In order to do this, you must contact the court to request traffic school;

· **Request Trial by Written Declaration** – Send a certified or registered letter postmarked no later than five days prior to the appearance date or come to the court on or before the appearance date to request a Trial by Written

Declaration and submit the bail amount. You will be given forms to allow you to write a statement and to submit other evidence without appearing in court. An officer will also submit a statement. The judge or judicial officer will consider the evidence and decide the case.

Paying the Ticket

Paying the ticket seems easy, right? You can just pay the ticket and get rid of the headache, right? Not necessarily. If you do pay the ticket, you have to worry about points being added to your driving record and an increase to your insurance rates. If you pay for the ticket and attend traffic school you have to waste your valuable time and more of your hard-earned money on the cost of attendance and the additional traffic school fees to the court. Fighting the ticket may be a better and smarter option for you.

Fighting the Ticket in Court

You can either contact the court or go to court on or before your arraignment date (the date written on the bottom of the ticket near your signature) and request a court trial at which the officer will probably be present. This is your first opportunity to get your ticket dismissed because if the officer doesn't show up, your ticket should be dismissed with no questions asked. However, if the officer does show up you will have to stand up and defend yourself before a judge. If that happens you may be too nervous or intimidated to accurately and compellingly tell your side of the story, providing logical reasons why the ticket should be dismissed.

GET DISMISSED: THE SEQUEL

What most people don't know is that they can avoid all this by fighting the ticket using a Trial by Written Declaration; a written document allows you to explain your side of the story from the comfort of your own home rather than a court trial in which it is necessary for both sides to appear before the judge. This will also allow you to ensure that you are able to tell your whole side of the story in writing, rather than struggling to remember what to say in front of a judge and hundreds of other people in court.

Fighting the Ticket by Trial by Written Declaration
By using a Trial by Written Declaration to fight your ticket you can say everything in writing that you had planned to say if you went to court. You can present your case to the judge in a well thought out manner and never have to step foot in the courtroom. The option for a Trial by Declaration is generally listed on the back of a ticket or on the courtesy notice you receive from the court.

There is no cost to file a Trial by Declaration with the court on your own, although you do need to remember that you still have to pay the bail amount (fine for your ticket) up front and wait for your ticket to be dismissed before you receive that money back from the court. The court will cash your bail check, but it will be held in trust pending the outcome of your case. If the court finds you not guilty your bail is refunded to you, your case is dismissed and there won't be any points added onto your driving record. If, based on your written story, the court believes you deserve only a partial dismissal they can reduce your fine or reduce the ticket to a non-moving violation. In the latter case, you would still have to pay a fine, but there won't be any points going on your record so there would be no need to attend traffic school. Often a ticket reduced to a zero-point non-moving violation is said to be "as good as a dismissal." This is especially true for commercial drivers who hold a professional Class "A" or "B" driver license and are not permitted to take traffic school in the same manner as a non-commercial driver.

GET DISMISSED: THE SEQUEL

It's Best to Fight That Traffic Ticket

Receiving a traffic ticket is a very frustrating experience and the thought of having to fight that ticket can make it even worse. However, as frustrating and complicated as it may seem, it's really not as bad as it sounds. In fact, once you've already received the ticket, it can only get better...by doing something about it with the GetDismissed service!

If you're like most people you've come to the conclusion that it's best for you to fight that traffic ticket. This is a great choice because no matter what type of ticket it is you should never give up your rights and just accept the ticket along with the hefty fine and point on your driving record. Always fight that traffic ticket!

We suggest an 8-step process when considering contesting a traffic ticket:

Step 1 – Know What You Were Cited For
First, ensure you were cited for a type of ticket that you can contest. To determine this, identify the type of ticket you were cited for, the court in which your ticket is filed, and

when your ticket is due. If you don't already know, or aren't sure, you need to identify whether the type of ticket you have involves a non-parking, moving violation such as a red light, stop sign, speeding, cell phone or other type of ticket.

Next, confirm that the ticket is filed with a Superior Court of California because tickets filed with the U.S. District Federal Court cannot be contested in writing using California's Trial by Written Declaration method. Finally, be sure that your ticket is still current and not past due because tickets that are past due or have gone to collections are no longer eligible to be contested using the Trial by Written Declaration defense.

Not all tickets are equal. Some can even be fixed with little effort and a small fee. Tickets for not having proof of insurance with you when you get pulled over, or for your front license plate not being mounted or any number of other "fixable" items are generally correctable but still involve you spending considerable amounts of time getting the problems corrected.

Here's how to tell if your violation is a correctable "fix-it ticket" versus a moving violation:

Check your ticket in the same area that you find the violation code; generally right around the center of the ticket. There are boxes on the left side and if the "Yes" box is checked then this violation is correctable.

GET DISMISSED: THE SEQUEL

If your traffic ticket is not a correctable violation then it is usually a traffic infraction that will likely apply at least one negative point on your driving record. Common types of traffic violations include:

• Speeding Ticket

• Red Light Ticket – as witnessed by an officer

• Red Light Photo Ticket - as received in the mail

• Sign Violations

• Carpool Violations

• U-Turn Violations

• Cell Phone Tickets

• Other Violation

Step 2 – Research Violation Code Listed on the Ticket

Now it's time to review your traffic ticket and identify the violation code. This is not always easy for the average person to identify; most do not know what the term violation code refers to and don't know where on the ticket to locate the code. The violation code on most tickets is found right in the middle of the ticket, below all your personal information like your name, address, vehicle information and insurance company. The violation code is usually accompanied by a subsection or possibly a subdivision and both pieces of information are equally important for you to have to ensure that you're referring to the correct law.

However, identifying the correct violation code is not always as cut and dry as some may have lost the ticket or cannot read the officer's writing. As an example, an unknown violation code for a speeding ticket can be determined by factoring in the speed limit, the cited speed, the type of vehicle being driven at the time, the class of driver license you have, the number of lanes on the highway you were driving on and the location (i.e. whether the violation occurred on a city street or a freeway).

Step 3 – Identify Whether the Violation is a Traffic Infraction or a Misdemeanor

In researching the violation code you must also determine whether you have been cited for a traffic infraction or a misdemeanor. Most people are not aware of the difference or what either term means. It is important to identify which one you were cited for so that you know your rights under the law and what penalties you might face if convicted.

A traffic infraction is a less serious offense such as speeding, red light, going through a stop sign, use of a cell phone while driving, and others. For a traffic infraction, you are allowed a traffic trial, either in person before a judge with your accuser, the officer, present or a Trial by Written Declaration. If you choose the latter and are found guilty after a Trial by Written Declaration you are allowed a new trial called a "trial de novo" and this is an person trial before a judge with the officer present. The penalties for a traffic infraction include fines but not jail time.

A misdemeanor, on the other hand, is a more serious offense and includes such items as driving while unlicensed, drunk driving, driving a grossly overweight truck, driving a commercial truck at 15 mph or more above the legal limit, and others. For these misdemeanors, you could face jail time in addition to a fine. Since you could potentially face jail time in some instances, you are allowed a trial by jury and to choose to have a court appointed public defender to help you if you can't afford your own lawyer.

You can look to the same area where the violation code is found and following the violation code there should be an 'I' or a 'M' circled. This tells you if you were cited for an infraction or misdemeanor and only traffic infractions can be fought using a Trial by Written Declaration.

Step 4 – Search for Any Exceptions to the Law
Once you have identified the violation code for the traffic infraction for which you were cited, you can get to work researching the applicable law related to that violation. There are often exceptions to each law that can be applied to an individual case. For example, the law states you cannot drive over double yellow lines. However, this is not an absolute law. You see, there are exceptions like turning into or out of a driveway, turning left at an intersection or making a U-turn.

You must always check for exceptions to the law because many times we find that officers tend to overlook these exceptions and issue a ticket when one was not justified in the first place.

Step 5 – Review Facts Surrounding the Incident
After you've taken the time to thoroughly research your violation, you need to review the facts of your case. Each violation is different and depending on the violation you were cited for there are certain details that will be more relevant than others. Plus, judges have a limited amount of time to spend reviewing your case and won't have the patience to thumb through pages of irrelevant details in order to get to the meat of the issue.

It's also important that you thoroughly look through, and eliminate, any insignificant details to get only the really important facts that will help get your ticket dismissed. All relevant details need to be carefully documented for use later and combined with your own independent research in preparing a proper statement for dismissal.

Step 6 – Apply Facts to Exceptions in the Law to Determine If Any Are Applicable
Now take the facts you have provided based on your best recollection of the day you received the ticket and compare the facts to any exceptions laid out in the law you were cited for. Any exceptions that are applicable should be noted for later use and to be combined with other possible defenses.

Step 7 – Research Possible Defenses and Review Similar Cases that Have Been Dismissed

Having the ability to review past traffic cases that have been dismissed may give you better knowledge as to what defenses tend to be successful with the court. Also determine if there are any other defenses that can be applied based on the facts of your case, such as if there was an emergency situation or other mitigating circumstance.

In every case you need to work to create doubt in the eyes of the court that the officer actually saw you breaking the law and to create doubt as to whether the officer's determination was accurate. For example, if you received a speeding ticket but provide details that at the time you were cited it was dark and the officer was preoccupied issuing a ticket to another motorist you can create enough reasonable doubt to show that the officer could not have correctly identified your speed.

Step 8 – Prepare a Trial by Written Declaration Statement Using All Applicable Defenses

The recommended method to contest a traffic ticket. This is the final step in fighting your ticket. Based on your independent research of the violation for which you were cited, together with the facts gathered, and using all defenses and exceptions to the law that you have found are applicable to your case, you're now ready to prepare a solid request for dismissal. You must use all this important, relevant, information to prepare a Trial by Written Declaration. The declaration along with all additional documentation and supporting evidence such as photographs or witness statements need to be submitted to the court.

So, there it is. You have it all. There are a lot of little details and know-how involved with properly preparing and filing a Trial by Written Declaration. You need to develop a good sense of what to say, what not to say, and what works. Now are you ready to put all those steps to work and start fighting your ticket?

Well, here's some great news: You don't have to be ready! The GetDismissed application can automate this process for you. Based on over a decade of traffic ticket knowledge and contesting California traffic tickets using a Trial by Written Declaration, the mystery and science behind this process has been uncovered and fully automated. Just take a picture of your traffic ticket and driver license, answer a few questions and your fully completed Trial by Written Declaration documents will be available for you to download, print and submit to the court to contest your traffic ticket.

The Best Way to Contest Your Traffic Ticket

If you want to fight your traffic ticket – and we think that you should – you have basically two options:

Contest your traffic ticket in court – This will either be time consuming, if you decide to do it on your own, or costly, if you decide to hire an attorney.

Of course, if you do go to court yourself be prepared for a frustrating experience. You will be in the courtroom with several hundred of your best friends, 75% of whom the bailiff will scare into blindly accepting traffic school. If you're one of the "fortunate" ones who decided to stay all day just to hear your name called and get to present your case to the judge, you better be prepared. This can be a full-day adventure.

As mentioned, you can always pay an attorney to do this for you. Just make sure you save up enough for a trip to Disneyland for a family of four or about $500 for attorney's fees. To get a good attorney, it can cost you a weekend in Vegas or up to $2,000. And even after spending all that money - there are no guarantees that your ticket will be dismissed. That is always up to the judge, and no attorney can guarantee a judge's decision.

OR...

You do have another option. A Trial by Written Declaration provides you the opportunity to contest your case in court without actually having to go to court. It's almost like winning the lottery. You can say everything you want to say without the fear of the judge throwing you out of the courtroom - because you never even have to go to court. This is a real court trial, just in written form instead of in person.

Some people believe that you don't need to know what to say, how to say it, or most importantly what not to say when filing a Trial by Written Declaration. This can't be further from the truth. There are many services out there, GetDismissed.com included, that provide assistance completing and filing a proper Trial by Written Declaration so that you are maximizing your chances of getting your traffic ticket dismissed.

If your Trial by Written Declaration is successful it will prevent a negative point from going on your driving record and the court will refund 100% of the bail you deposited with them. Almost as good, a Trial by Declaration has one other advantage: you are allowed to take "two bites of the apple." This means that, even in a worst-case scenario (for example, if you are found guilty on a Trial by Written Declaration), you actually still get to have your day in court by filing a Trial de Novo (the request for a new trial). This will put you right back where you started, meaning you can still go to court to contest your traffic ticket; that's the proverbial second bite of the apple.

Now you can see why the best way to contest a traffic ticket in California is with a Trial by Written Declaration; it saves you time and money! Not to mention you still retain all your rights under the law for a court trial if you so desire. And let's not forget that GetDismissed.com and the GetDismissed mobile application make this process as simple and easy as possible. So GetDismissed to help your ticket...get dismissed!

History of a Trial by Written Declaration
California courts are extremely over-crowded. Every time someone comes to court to contest a traffic ticket, it takes up valuable court time and money. In 1978 California began a new program in an effort to free up court time while still allowing individuals all the rights afforded to them under the law. California created a "Trial by Written Declaration" as a way to free up the court's time and save the court money.

A Trial by Written Declaration will allow you to contest your traffic ticket without the need to actually go to court. If the ticket is dismissed then no points will be added to your record and the court will refund your bail in full. If your ticket is not dismissed you can still either request traffic school, if you are eligible, or request a new trial in the courtroom to contest your ticket again.

Doesn't this make sense now? Contesting a traffic ticket in California with a Trial by Written Declaration is your best option to fight your traffic ticket and keep your driving record clean, which in turn saves you money on auto insurance premiums. If you win and your traffic ticket is dismissed, no points go on your driving record and your bail is fully refunded. If it's not dismissed, no harm is done and you're right back where you started prior to filing a Trial by Written Declaration. Either way you just can't lose!

It makes total sense for anyone who receives a traffic ticket in the State of California to file a Trial by Written Declaration first, instead of wasting their time going to court, attending traffic school, or just paying the fine.

The beauty of a Trial by Declaration is that even if your ticket is not dismissed fully or reduced to your liking, you can still ask for the new trial by filing form TR-220 with the court within 20 days of the court finding you guilty. At the new trial, you will have to appear in court but this still gives you a fresh start and a second opportunity at getting your ticket dismissed. This is considered a completely new trial.

Remember a Trial by Declaration does not require your appearance in court. A new trial on the other hand will, if it comes to that. Hopefully your ticket will be dismissed and you won't ever have to worry about a new trial. After filing your Trial by Written Declaration with the court it will take about 30-90 days to hear back from the court. Once the court receives your Trial by Written Declaration, the court notifies the officer by mailing the officer an officer's declaration.

GET DISMISSED: THE SEQUEL

The officer is given a date by which to respond back and upon arrival of that date the judge will review the declarations and then render a decision. It's as simple as that.

Simple as the Trial by Written Declaration process is, there are still some things you need to know. For example, knowing what to leave out of your Trial by Written Declaration statement can be even more important than knowing what to put into it.

How to Determine if You Are Eligible for a Trial by Written Declaration

Just about anyone can file a Trial by Written Declaration with a few exceptions. For example, to be eligible to file a Trial by Written Declaration, you need to be over the age of 18. If you were under 18 when you got the ticket most courts require that you have your parent or guardian request a Trial by Written Declaration on your behalf. If you were cited for not having a valid driver license or for driving on a suspended or expired license you generally cannot file a Trial by Written Declaration either.

You must have a traffic ticket that includes a traffic infraction - not a misdemeanor. Speeding tickets, red light camera tickets, lane violation tickets, stop sign tickets and other traffic infractions will all qualify.

However, drunk driving, driving without a valid license or driving on a suspended driver license, tickets resulting from accidents, and other misdemeanors do not qualify.

In addition, your traffic violation must not require a mandatory court appearance. If your traffic violation does require a mandatory court appearance, you will need to appear in court on or before the date indicated on the ticket, and request the judge to set bail and allow you to file a Trial by Written Declaration. If the judge allows you to do this you can proceed with a Trial by Written Declaration process as discussed previously.

Tickets that are not eligible for a Trial by Written Declaration include: parking tickets, administrative tickets, tickets issued by park rangers, and other tickets that are not on file with the California Superior Court, such as tickets filed in U.S. District Courts; none of those are eligible. Additionally, tickets that are past their due date or that have been referred to a collections agency are no longer eligible for a Trial by Written Declaration.

How to Ask the Court for a Trial by Written Declaration
When filing a Trial by Written Declaration the court must receive your documents and bail no later than the due date of your ticket. We recommend that you get all your documents to the court within 5 days of your specified due date, to ensure that the court receives everything on time and records it in their system. By doing so you will avoid any

possibility of receiving an FTA - or Failure to Appear - for not showing up on your court date.

It is not necessary to go to the court to file a Trial by Written Declaration. Since the Trial by Written Declaration procedure doesn't require you to actually go to the courthouse to submit your documents, it is recommended you send all of your documents by certified mail instead of regular mail. Sending your documents by certified mail guarantees that you have an acknowledgement that the court actually received your documents and the date on which they were received.

You must file your Trial by Written Declaration documents with the courthouse indicated at the bottom of the ticket or to the address that is indicated on your courtesy notice.

Don't delay in taking care of your traffic ticket! Remember what we said about tickets that have not been taken care of; if they are past due or have been referred to collections then you can't request a Trial by Written Declaration.

How to File a Trial by Written Declaration

The first step of this process is to obtain the Trial by Written Declaration documents. You can obtain these documents by going to www.GetDismissed.com or any Superior Court web site.

A Trial by Written Declaration is a two-page document. The first page (see Figure 1) contains basic information about the court-house, the bail amount of your ticket and the due date of the ticket.

TR-205

NAME OF COURT: Superior Court of California, County of Los Angeles
STREET ADDRESS: 1725 Main Street, Room 214
MAILING ADDRESS:
CITY AND ZIP CODE: Santa Monica-90401
BRANCH NAME: West District

FOR COURT USE ONLY

PEOPLE OF THE STATE OF CALIFORNIA
vs.
DEFENDANT: Jane Doe

REQUEST FOR TRIAL BY WRITTEN DECLARATION
(Vehicle Code, § 40902)

TO BE FILLED OUT BY COURT CLERK

CITATION NUMBER: C1234567

CASE NUMBER:

A. DUE DATE (for receipt of this form and any unpaid bail) *(specify)*:
08/24/2015

B. Bail amount required: $

C. Bail amount already deposited by defendant: $

D. Date mailed or delivered by clerk:

E. Mail or deliver completed form, evidence, and mail to the Clerk of the *(specify)*: Santa Monica Court at (mailing *address*):
1725 Main Street, Room 214
Santa Monica-90401

REQUEST FOR TRIAL

1. I have reviewed the Instructions to *Defendant* (Trial by *Written Declaration*) (form TR-200).
2. I request to have a trial by written declaration.
3. The facts contained in the Declaration of Facts on the reverse are personally known to me and are true and correct.
4. I know that I have the right not to be compelled to be a witness against myself. I understand and agree that by making any statement, I am giving up and waiving that right and privilege.
5. EVIDENCE The following evidence supports my case and includes everything I want the court to consider in deciding my case:
   - a. ☐ photographs (specify *total* number):
   - b. ☐ medical record
   - c. ☐ registration documents
   - d. ☐ inspection certificate
   - e. ☐ diagram
   - f. ☐ car repair receipt
   - g. ☐ insurance documents
   - h. ☐ other *(specify)*:

(Declaration continued on reverse)

Form Adopted by the Judicial Council of California TR-205 [New January 1, 1999]

REQUEST FOR TRIAL BY WRITTEN DECLARATION
(Trial by Written Declaration-Traffic)

Vehicle Code, § 40902

Figure 1: *First page of a Trial by Written Declaration document*

As you can see most of the information required can be found either on your actual ticket or the courtesy notice the court sends you.

If you are including any additional evidence with your Trial by Written Declaration, such as photographs, you need to check the appropriate box at the bottom of the page shown above.

Please note items "B-D" on the Trial by Written Declaration. One major requirement of a Trial by Written Declaration is that you post your bail with the court when filing a Trial by Written Declaration. Since you will not be going to court to contest your traffic ticket the court requires you to post your bail in order for the court to consider your Trial by Written Declaration.

When the court receives your documents, they will cash your bail check and put it in the court's client trust account. If your ticket is dismissed your bail will be refunded to you in the form of a court check. If your ticket is not dismissed they will convert your bail to the fine for the ticket and close your case.

The second page of the Trial by Written Declaration is the "Statement of Facts" and can be seen in Figure 2:

PEOPLE v. DEFENDANT (Name):	CASE NUMBER:
Jane Doe	C1234567

6. DECLARATION OF FACTS *(Type or print only. State what happened and explain all the items of evidence you checked in Item 5 on the reverse and tell how they support your case. You may add additional pages.)*

(Name): Jane Doe

(Current mailing address):
1313 Mockingbird Lane
Beverly Hills, CA 91902

STATEMENT OF FACTS *(begin here):*

See attached

7. Number of pages attached: __3__

I declare under penalty of perjury under the laws of the State of California that the foregoing is true and correct.

Date:

Jane Doe

(TYPE OR PRINT NAME)   ▶ _____
                                                        (SIGNATURE)

Figure 2: Second page of a Trial by Written Declaration

At the top of the page you must put your full legal name and your case or citation number. After that you will indicate your mailing address. This is the address to which you would like the court to send any communications, including your decision notice. This address does not have to be the same as the address on your driver license. It should however be an address at which the mail is checked on a regular basis.

Next comes your actual Statement of Facts. This is where you will present your case to the court. Keep in mind that there is only a small space here but you can attach additional pages as necessary to fully explain your case properly. You should make sure that you present your case in a clear and concise manner. Take the time to make your points clearly but do not run on excessively as the court will lose interest.

If you do need to attach additional pages, be sure to put your name and case or citation number at the top of each page and the page number at the bottom of each page.

What to Include in a Trial by Written Declaration and What Not to Include

As we touched upon before, any Trial by Written Declaration will include a Statement of Facts. Here you should begin by briefly summarizing what exactly you were cited for and include all relevant facts including anything important about the driving conditions at the time you were pulled over, such as the weather and the traffic. You can tell your side of the story and also bring up any possible defenses. You must include a thorough discussion of any photographs, diagrams, or witness statements you plan to include with the Trial by Declaration documents; photos, diagrams and witness statements can be helpful to your case.

If you were cited for more than one violation on the same ticket, remember to include a discussion about all violations in the same declaration document. If you were cited for more than one violation but they are listed on different tickets, you will need to prepare and submit separate Trial by Written Declaration documents for each ticket.

Remember you don't have to include every single detail and you should avoid putting in details which might have a negative impact. For example, if you were cited for traveling too fast on a city street you would probably want to mention that there were no pedestrians or parks nearby; but if there were pedestrians and a park nearby you are better off not mentioning it. If you were cited for speeding on a freeway but you were being passed by other vehicles, you would definitely want to mention this to show how much more reasonable your speed was compared to the other motorists around you.

However, if you were the one passing all the other cars then it's in your best interest not to bring that up. If there was some sort of emergency situation that explains why you did what you did resulting in the ticket, then you will have to really consider just how significant this "emergency" was. On one hand, a judge may sympathize with you. On the other hand, you are admitting guilt. So, if it's something that was not truly an emergency, like needing to go to the bathroom, that excuse is probably not going to be very effective in getting your ticket dismissed.

At all costs please avoid antagonizing the officer who pulled you over! No matter how angry you may be about getting a ticket, this will not help gain a judge's sympathy and in fact may even irritate the judge. If you feel strongly that the officer's behavior was inappropriate during the course of your interaction, then you do have the right to file a complaint with the Police Department through which the officer is employed. The judge reviewing your Trial by Written Declaration statement is neither interested in hearing about the officer's bad manners nor unnecessary details. Be complete in your explanation and reasoning but also be succinct.

The average time a judge spends reviewing a Trial by Declaration statement is five to ten minutes. That's why you need to present your Trial by Declaration statement in a neat and organized fashion and include only those facts and details which are truly relevant. Conclude your declaration statement by respectfully requesting that the court dismiss the ticket in its entirety.

The GetDismissed.com web site and the GetDismissed mobile application have been developed to make this process easy for you.

GET DISMISSED: THE SEQUEL

How To Use the GetDismissed App

Ready for us to get to the point and tell you everything you need to know about using the GetDismissed mobile app? Let's get to it!

The most important thing to remember is that using the app is SIMPLE. We designed it specifically to make usage as quick, easy, and simple as possible because you've already got enough to worry about; you just got a ticket! But don't worry about that because you're just a few screen taps away from fighting that ticket.

The GetDismissed app is available for all iOS based devices in the Apple App Store and for all Android based devices in Google Play. Your first step is to download the app for your particular type of phone, either iPhone or Android or use our web app on your computer or mobile phone just by going to www.GetDismissed.com. Once you've downloaded the proper app you're ready for the next step.

Step two is to open the app on your phone or with your web browser and select "NEW USERS – TAP HERE TO SET UP YOUR ACCOUNT." (See Figure 3.) It's right about in the center of the screen; you really can't miss it. Of course, if you already have an account, just select "ALREADY HAVE AN ACCOUNT? TAP HERE TO SIGN IN". That's how SIMPLE this whole thing is.

Once you've set up your account, you will have 6 options (See Figure 4.) as follows:

1. Add Ticket

2. Get Membership

3. Your Details

4. Ticket History

5. Learn More

6. Notification

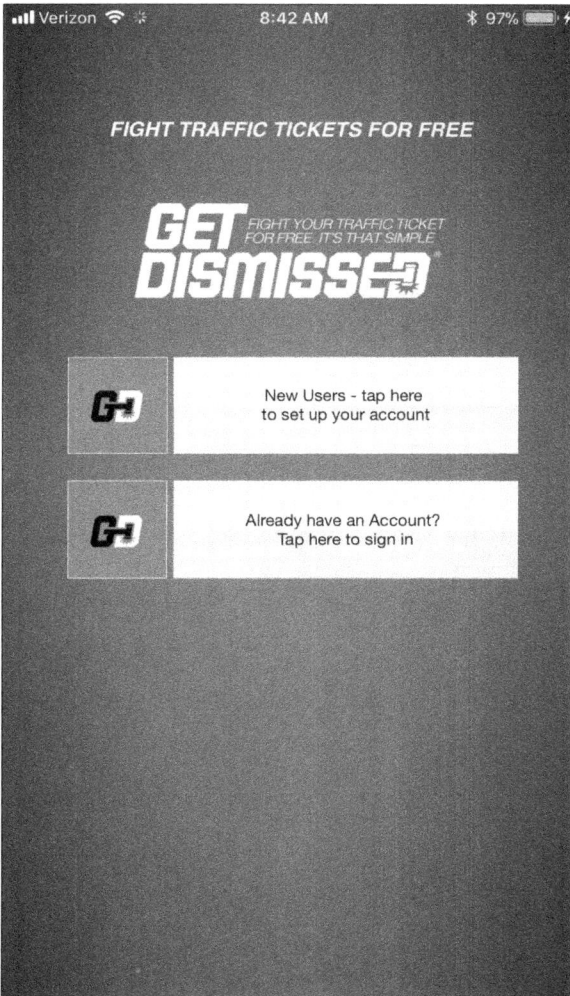

Figure 3: *New users set up account – Already have an account, sign in*

GET DISMISSED: THE SEQUEL

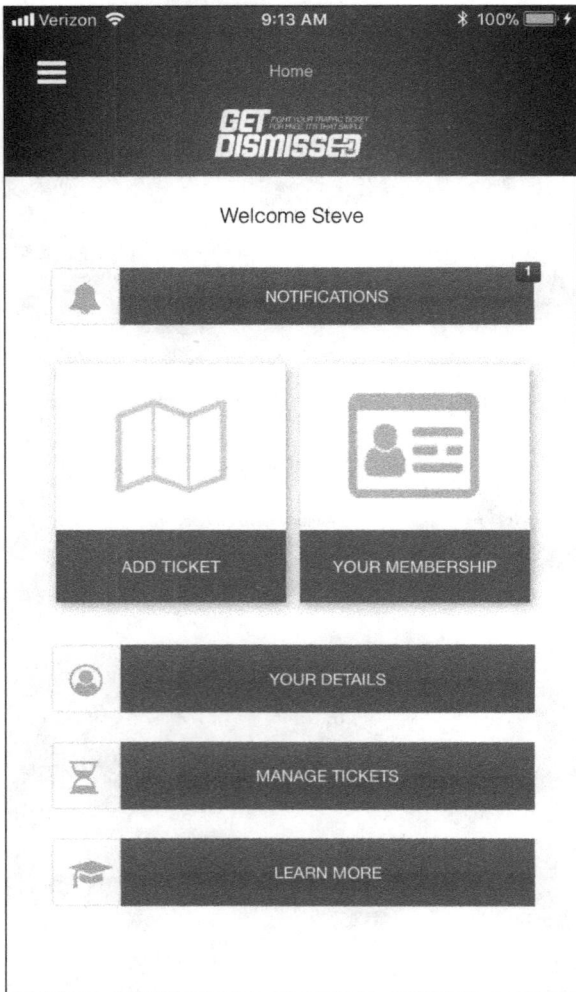

Figure 4: GetDismissed menu options

Add Ticket

Next, you're going to take a nice clean picture of your traffic ticket. The key here is clarity. We need to be able to see and read the information on the ticket, so use the brackets on your phone's screen as a guide. Don't worry about the background or whether the image is perfectly straight. The important part is our ability to get the information from the traffic ticket image.

You will then input the basic information about your ticket including:

- Type of ticket;

- Citation number;

- Courthouse; and

- Due Date

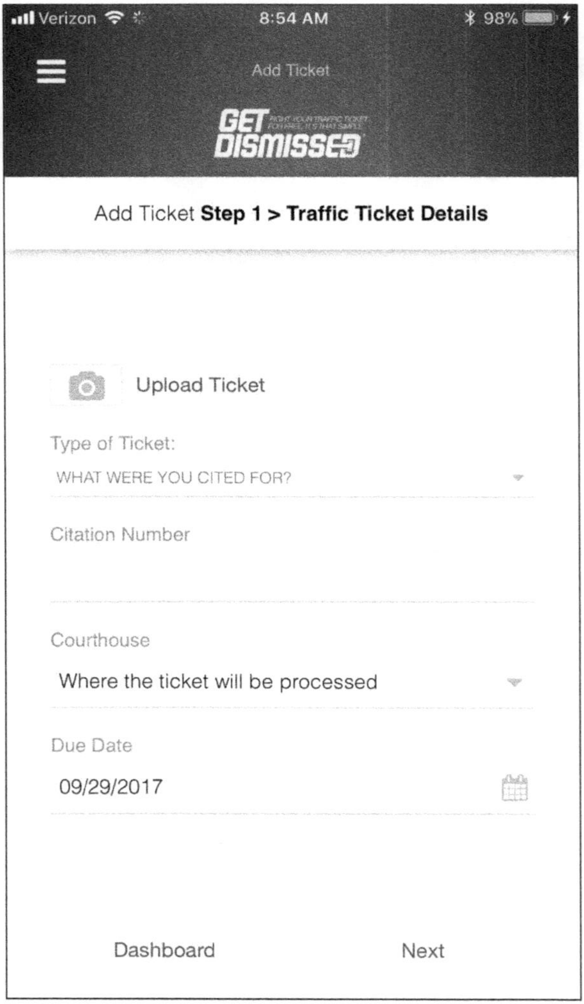

Figure 5: *Traffic ticket details and picture of traffic ticket*

GET DISMISSED: THE SEQUEL

We know you want GetDismissed to work so please follow the next important part carefully. What will happen next is that you will tap through a short series of menus that describe your particular type of ticket (See Figures 6 and 7). For example, if you received a speeding ticket the app will ask you; "How did the officer measure your speed?" And then a series of possible options will let you select the correct choice.

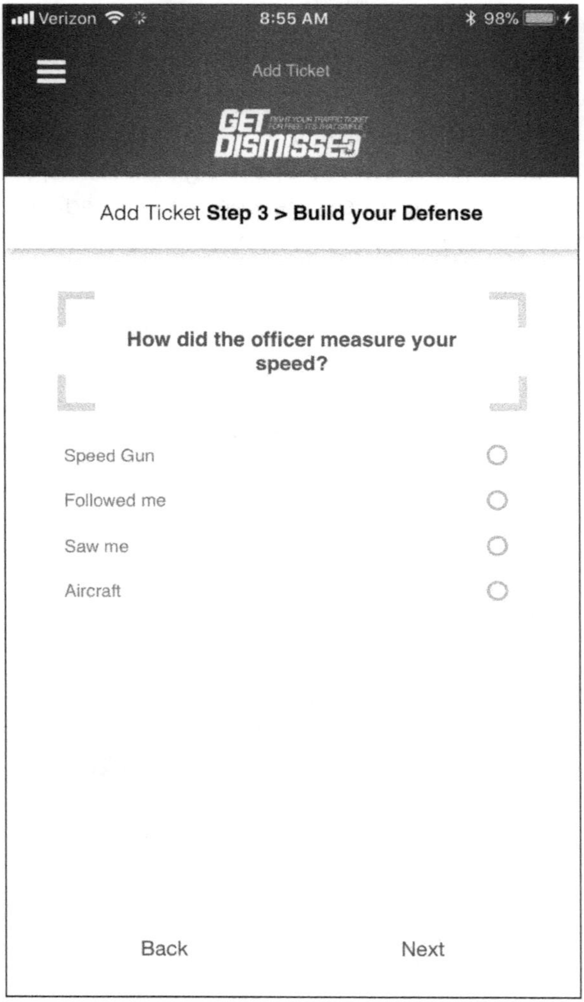

Figure 6: The app will ask you for details about your ticket

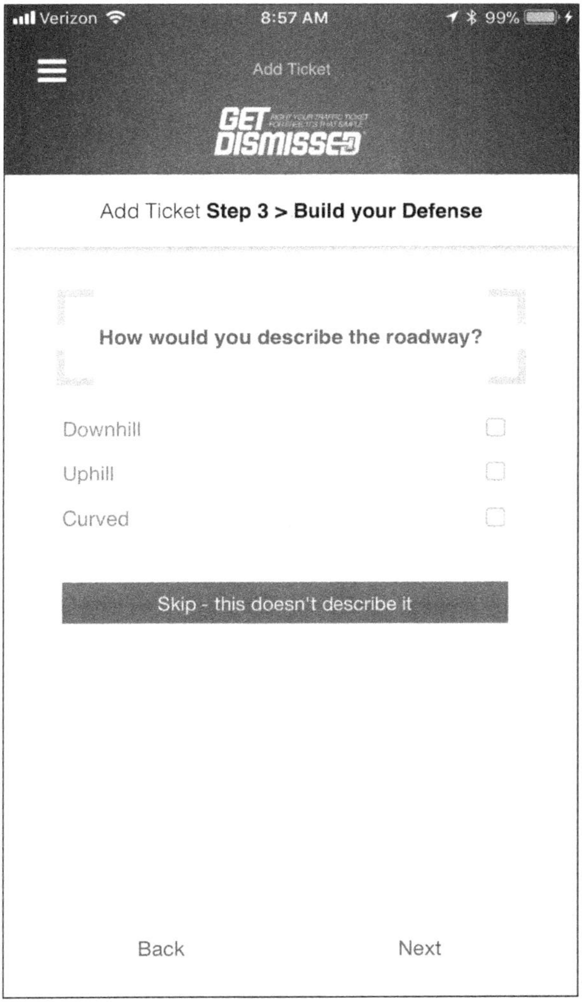

Figure 7: The app will ask you for further details about your ticket

GET DISMISSED: THE SEQUEL

Options will include: "Speed Gun," "Followed Me," "Saw Me," and "Aircraft." IT'S THAT SIMPLE!

Once we know what type of ticket you've been issued we can start building your case, so you can fight your traffic ticket, get it dismissed, and save money! After you've made and selected all the choices in the prior incident type menu, we now need you to tell us why the officer should not have ticketed you. To do that we need just a few details about what happened. Another series of choices will appear with options suited to your ticket type (See Figure 8). Let's stick with the speeding ticket example: in this case the "Incident Details" menu will provide choices and images such as: "Darkness," "Bad Weather,""Other Cars in the Way," and "Large Distance Between You and the Officer." Make all the choices that apply. But remember these have to be accurate because once you submit your Trial by Declaration paperwork to court, the officer who issued the ticket is going to have a chance to respond with his side of the story. You wouldn't want to argue that it was too "dark" for the officer to see you clearly when the judge will read the officer's paperwork and see that the ticket was issued in broad daylight would you?

WAIT! Before you go on, take a minute to review your case details and summary (see Figure 9) and make sure all your information is correct. This is your chance to make any changes or corrections to your prior choices. Done? Good. Now we can move on.

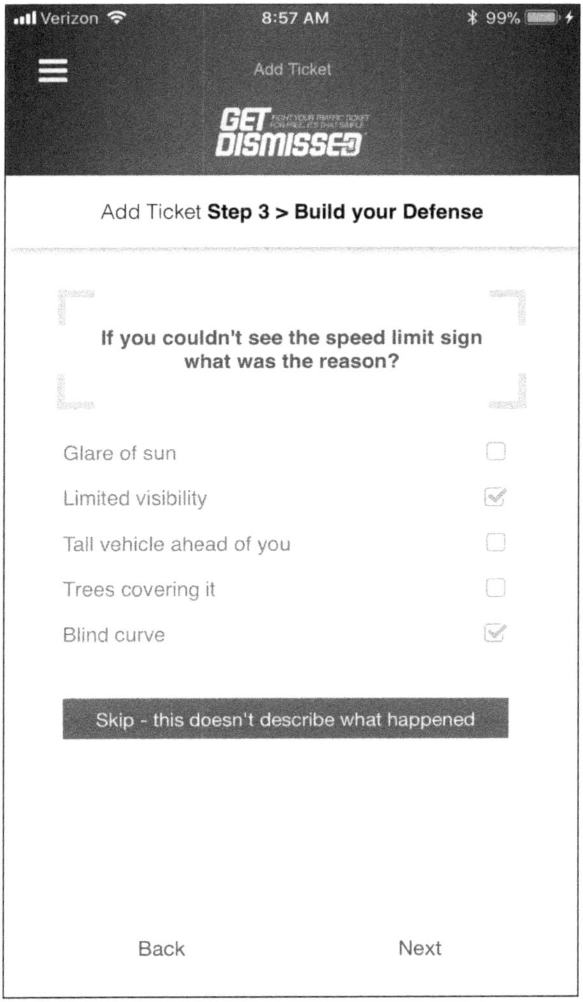

Figure 8: The app will prompt you for circumstances that are important for building your case

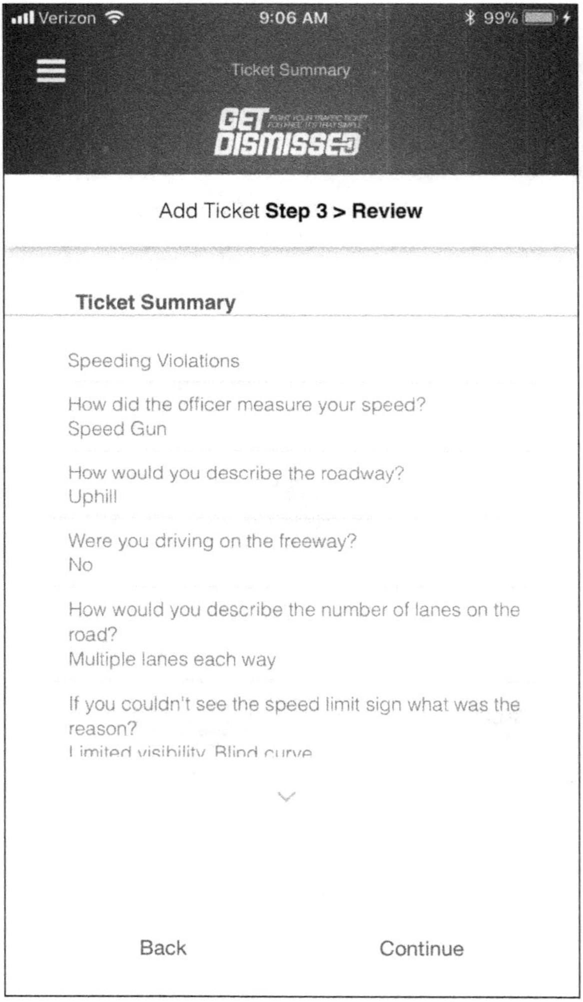

Figure 9: *Review your ticket summary to make sure everything is correct*

The Final Step: Proceed to Checkout.

The Checkout screen will have the amount or "Cost of Service" required for GetDismissed to put together your entire Trial by Declaration case. Also on this screen you will be asked to enter your credit or debit card number, billing details, and a few pieces of other information needed to process your payment. (See Figures 10-12)

Once that's all filled in just tap the "Make Payment" button and TAA-DAA! You're almost done.

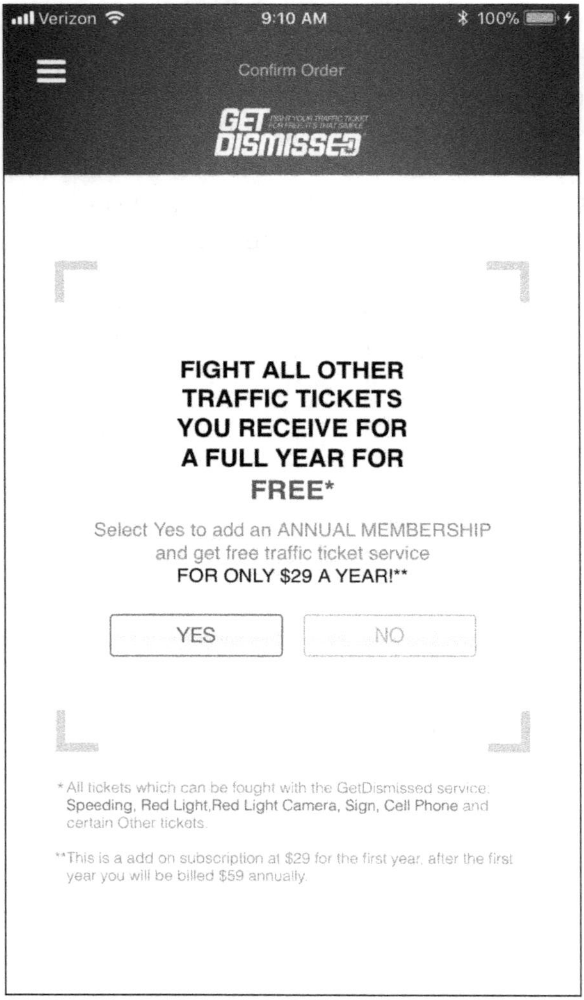

Figure 10: *At checkout, you will be prompted to add a membership so you can fight future tickets for FREE*

GET DISMISSED: THE SEQUEL

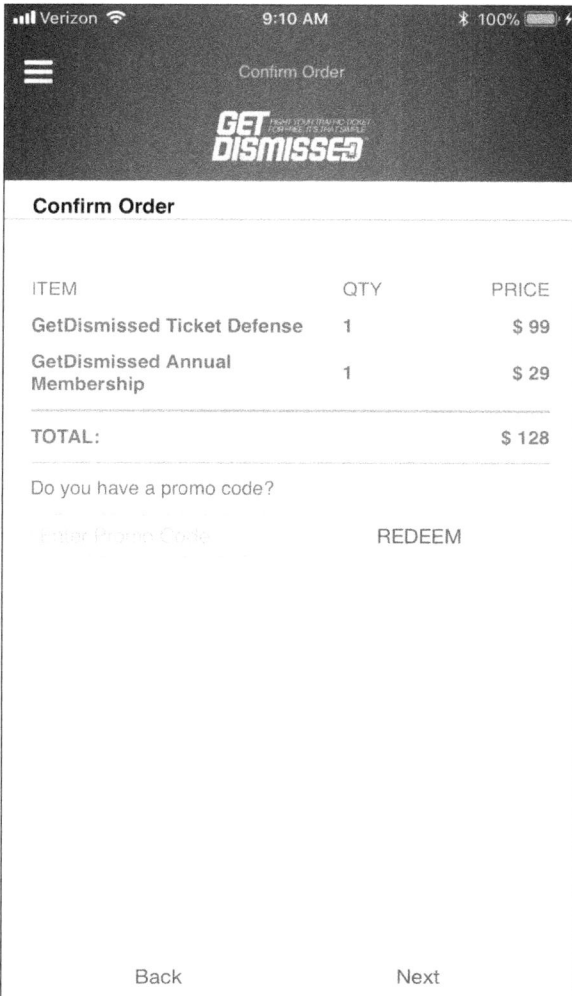

Figure 11: You can now review your order prior to payment

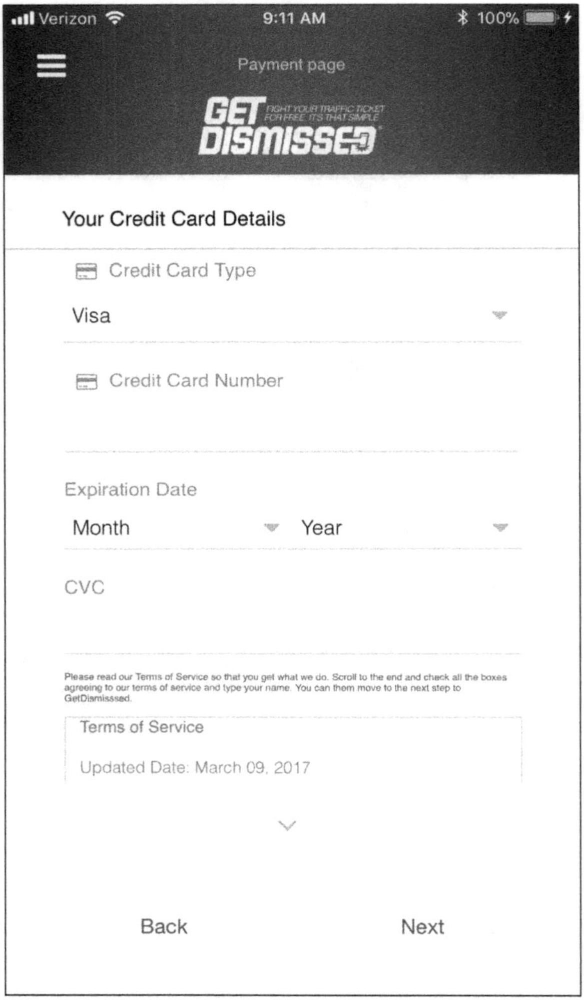

Figure 12: *Enter your billing information and payment information*

GET DISMISSED: THE SEQUEL

Shortly after your payment has been processed you will receive two emails from GetDismissed so be sure to check your email account frequently (See Figure 13). The first email will be your receipt of payment. This receipt will also have your GetDismissed account information and login information, so please hold onto this...just in case you ever need to reference the order.

You will not receive the second email until we have completed your Trial by Written Declaration and all your defense documents. This email will have a link to your account and case documents when they are completed; you can also choose to get a text message with this link. Click on the link and print out all of the pages. NOW you have just two steps left to go: Get a bail check and get a stamp.

California law requires you to post bail with your Trial by Declaration paperwork. Remember the court will refund you 100% of the bail amount if your ticket gets dismissed. You'll just need to get a check and make it payable to the court for the bail amount specified by the court; you can get the amount from the court's website or the notice you received in the mail from the court. Include that check with the Trial by Declaration case paperwork you just printed out, then get a stamp and mail it to the courthouse indicated on the ticket. AND NOW YOU'RE DONE! See, we told you it was simple.

Remember just because you're fighting your ticket using the Trial by Declaration method it doesn't mean you've given up your right to confront the officer and see a judge face-to-face. Even if you lose the Trial by Declaration you can still go into court and have a whole new trial with a judge. You've lost almost nothing by using the GetDismissed App!

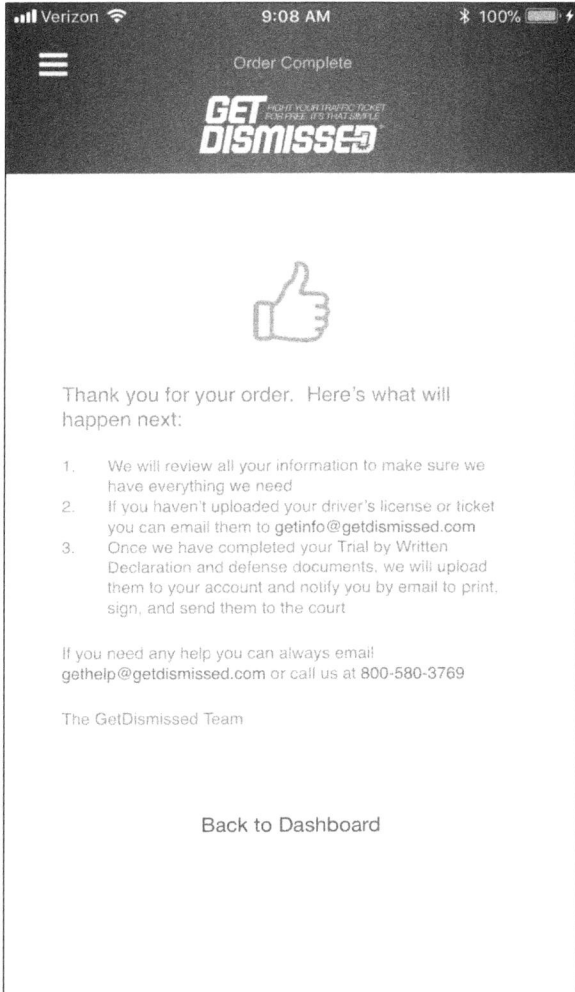

Figure 13: Thank you for your order

GET DISMISSED: THE SEQUEL

Get Membership (See Figure 14.)

There's no other membership program like the GetDismissed Membership program. If you drive in California, you need this membership to protect your driving record. With a GetDismissed membership you can fight most California traffic tickets you receive in the next 12 months for FREE including:

• Speeding Tickets;

• Red Light and Red-Light Camera Tickets;

• Cell Phone Tickets;

• Sign Tickets;

• Carpool Tickets;

• U-Turn Tickets;

• Commercial Driver Defenses;

• And Many More

There are also other benefits include with a GetDismissed Membership including:

• Free Traffic School;

• Free Insurance Review;

GET DISMISSED: THE SEQUEL

- The GetDismissed Ticket Newsletter;

- And Many Other Benefits

We do the best we can, however not every ticket is dismissed by the court. If you are found guilty, it's not a problem. We have arranged for all GetDismissed members that are eligible for traffic school to take it for FREE. This is a fantastic benefit of membership. You can't go wrong; Either the ticket will be dismissed or you will get to take traffic school for free with the GetDismissed program.

All GetDismissed members now can receive the lowest auto and home insurance rates available through our exclusive GetDismissed member insurance program.

Get This! You will also receive our weekly Traffic Ticket eNewsletter. You automatically opt-in to our eNewsletter when you have a GetDismissed Membership.

So go ahead, get your membership. Just fill out the information in the membership section of our app and bam, you now are covered for the next 12 months.

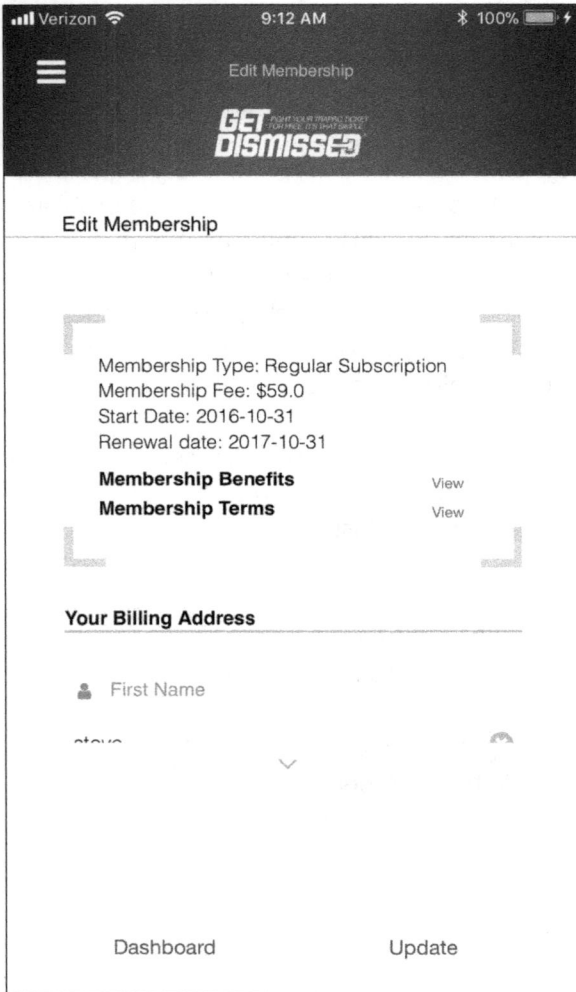

Figure 14: *GetDismissed membership information*

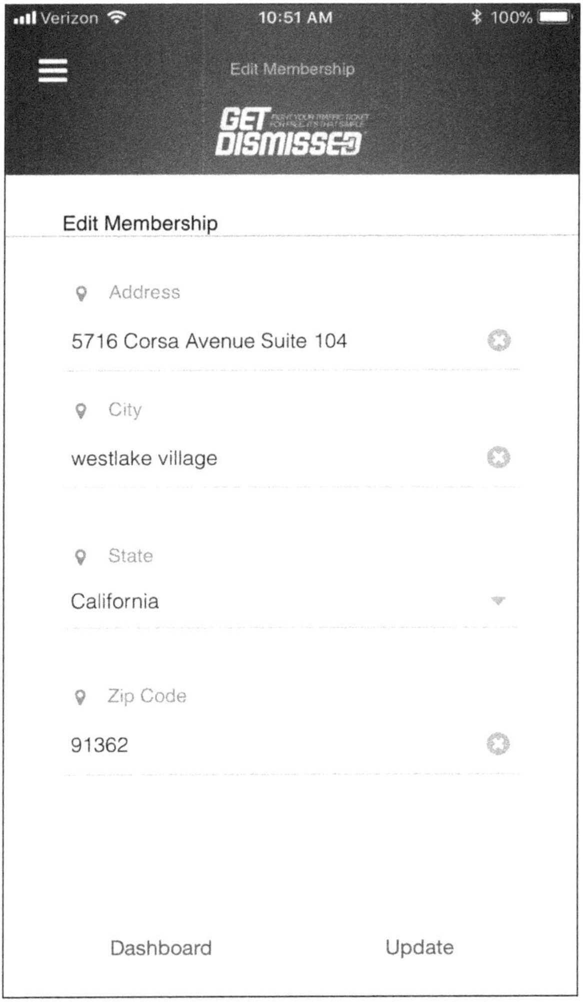

Figure 15: *More membership information*

Your Details

All your information is kept in this section. Keep it up to date. If anything changes like your mailing address, phone number, or email, just update it here. It's that simple.

You're also going to take a nice clean picture of your driver's license. The key here, again, is clarity. We need to be able to see and read the information on your license, so use the brackets on your phone's screen as a guide. Don't worry about the background or whether the image is perfectly straight. The important part is our ability to get the information from the driver's license image.

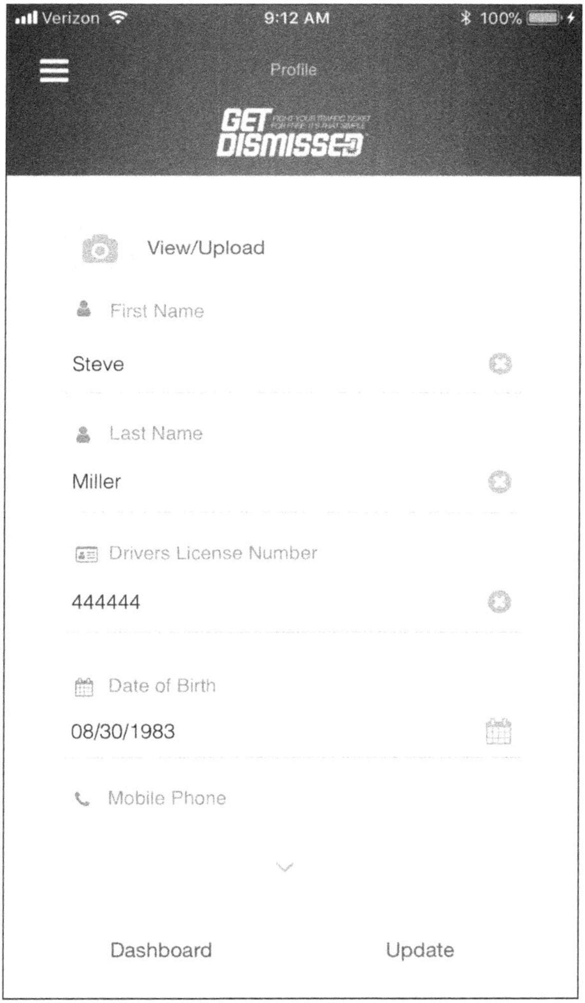

Figure 16: Your detail and clear photo of the front of your driver license

GET DISMISSED: THE SEQUEL

Ticket History

Like many drivers, you may receive several tickets over time. The Ticket History section is where you will go to manage all your tickets that you process through GetDismissed. You will see a list of all your tickets and you can just select view next to the ticket you would like to manage (See Figures 17 & 18).

Once you have select the ticket you would like to manage you will be able to do the following:

1. View/sign the Notice to Consumer;

2. View/sign our Terms and Conditions;

3. View/upload a copy of your ticket;

4. Edit/view all your ticket details;

5. Edit/view all your driver details;

6. Edit/view the ticket questionnaire;

7. View/print your completed Trial by Written Declaration and Defense documents; or

8. Process your GetDismissed payment

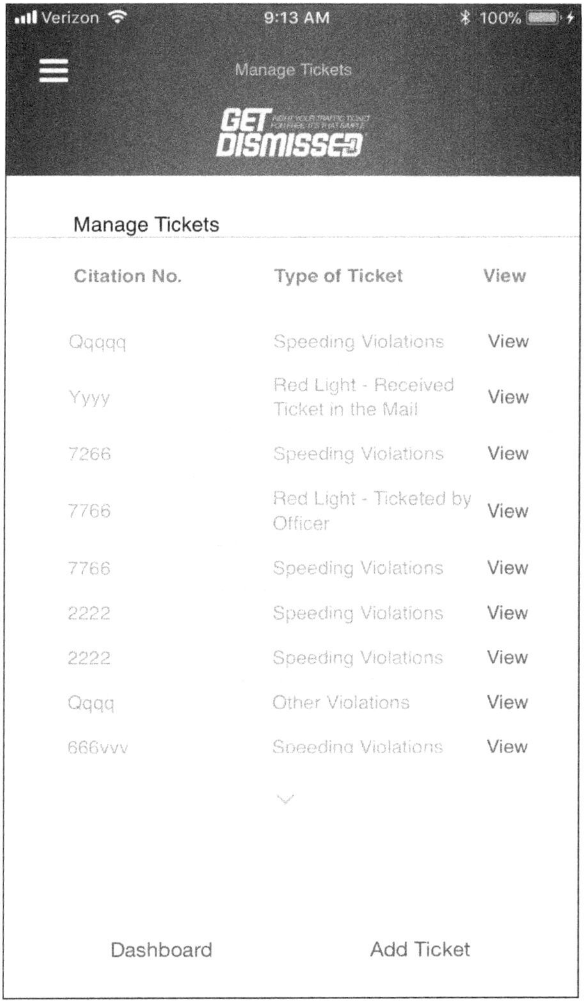

Figure 17: History of all your tickets

GET DISMISSED: THE SEQUEL

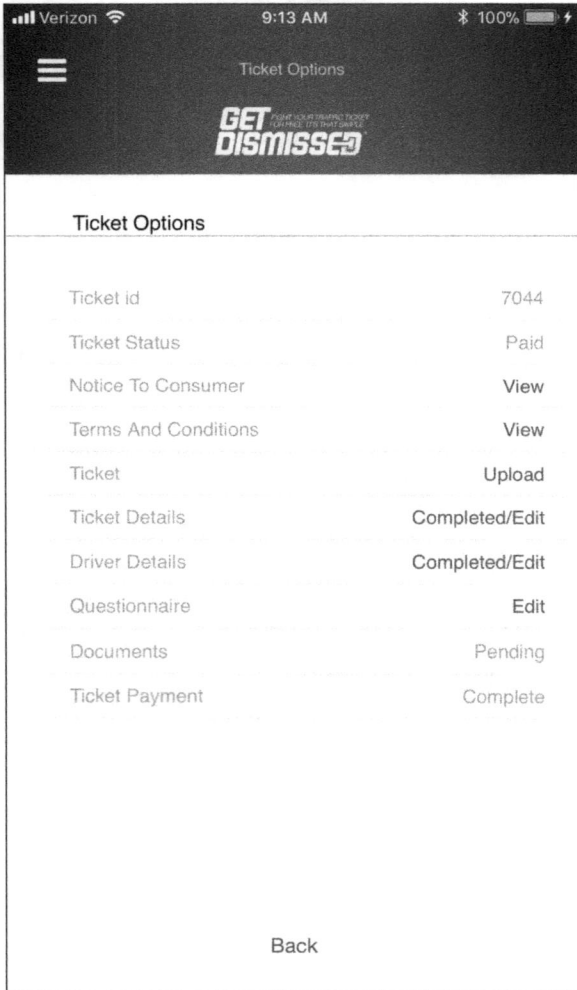

Figure 18: Manage all your ticket options

Learn More

Want more information about GetDismissed, no problem. Check out the "Learn More" section and read about our service and how you can fight your California traffic ticket and win, with a Trial by Written Declaration.

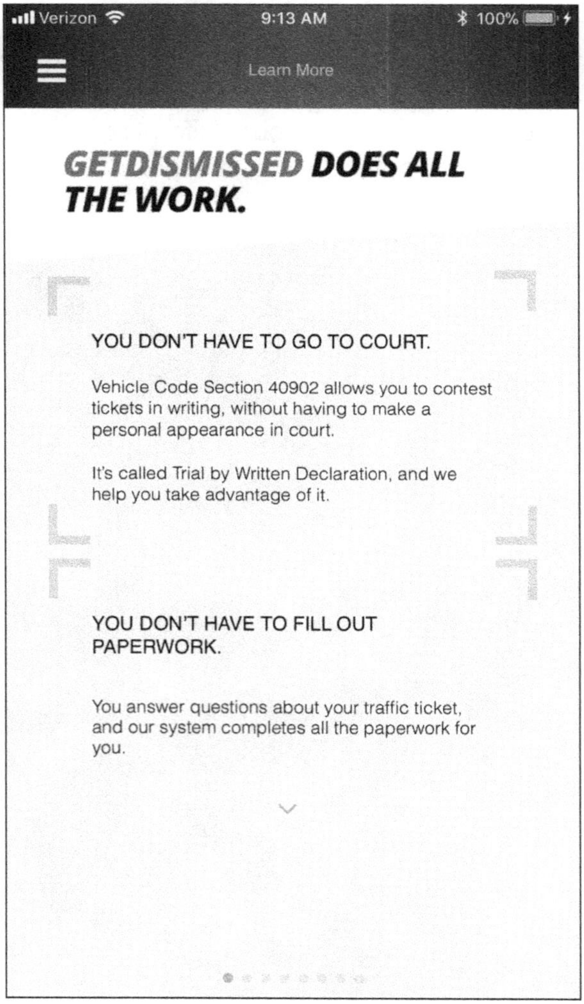

> .ıll Verizon 📶   9:13 AM   * 100% 🔋 ⚡
>
> ☰   Learn More
>
> ## *GETDISMISSED DOES ALL THE WORK.*
>
> ### YOU DON'T HAVE TO GO TO COURT.
>
> Vehicle Code Section 40902 allows you to contest tickets in writing, without having to make a personal appearance in court.
>
> It's called Trial by Written Declaration, and we help you take advantage of it.
>
> ### YOU DON'T HAVE TO FILL OUT PAPERWORK.
>
> You answer questions about your traffic ticket, and our system completes all the paperwork for you.
>
> ⌄

Figure 19: Learn More

GET DISMISSED: THE SEQUEL

Well there you have it; the GetDismissed app in a nutshell. That ticket isn't going to dismiss itself. So what are you waiting for? Get the app, sign up for a membership and get your ticket dismissed with GetDismissed!

GET DISMISSED: THE SEQUEL

Distracted Driving – You're Still Using Your Phone While Driving

Any activity that could divert a person's attention away from the primary task of driving. All distractions endanger driver, passenger, and bystander safety.

- Types of Distracted Driving

  - **Visual** – Taking your eyes of the road

  - **Manual** – Taking your hands off the wheel

  - **Cognitive** – Taking your mind off driving

There are also many other forms of distracted driving that can also be ticketable offenses. Check out the list below, are you guilty of any of these?

- Putting on make-up

- Shaving

- Disciplining kids in back seat

- Eating while driving

GET DISMISSED: THE SEQUEL

- Reading, including maps

- Using your navigation system

- Watching a video

- Distracted driving tickets

    - **Cell phone** – no points, just a fine. First ticket averages about $160 and all additional tickets average about $250

        - Violation codes

            - 23123a

            - 23123.5a

            - 23124b

    - **Other distracted driving tickets** – can carry a point and cost between $150 and $1,000 as a driver can be ticketed for "willful or wanton disregard for the safety of persons or property". This can also carry jail time, criminal charges and a civil lawsuit if it causes a crash.

- Typically charged for reckless driving code section 23103

Between the hefty fines, disturbing PSAs and social shunning that comes from using your phone while driving, it turns out nearly everyone is still texting, tweeting and generally fiddling with their phones while behind the wheel. According to Zendrive's extensive 3-month study of three million US drivers, we're using our phones at least once during 88% of our trips. That's not good.

The study analyzed 570 million trips over 5.6 billion miles and determined that on average, we used our phones instead of paying attention to the road for 3.5 minutes every hour. The state with the most distracted drivers was Vermont and the least distracted was Oregon. Both have hand-held phone bans. The most distracted city was Los Angeles, while California as a whole was one of the least distracted states.

With motor vehicle deaths up 6% in 2016 from 2015, and 14% from 2014 to 2016, this study is a stark reminder that while automobiles are getting safer, drivers are actually getting worse behind the wheel. Taking your eyes off the road for just two seconds increases the possibility of a crash 24 times. It takes an average of five seconds to text, during which a car traveling at 55 miles per hour can cover an entire football field.

Since the original hands-free law was enacted over 10 years ago much has changed. Think about all these current phone features that weren't even available 10 years ago:

• Listening to music;

• Taking pictures and selfies;

- Mobile applications;

- Facebook, Twitter, Instagram, and SnapChat;

- Instant messaging;

- Directions and maps;

- Stock quotes;

- Videos and movies;

- Mobile payment solutions;

- Financial management; and

- Ordering coffee with Starbucks mobile app

Yes, in 10 short years time cell phones sure have changed. The original hands-free laws could never have anticipated all this technology and all the different ways that people would try to use their mobile phones while driving. It was time to make a change to the law.

Prior to 2017, the law stated that you couldn't use your mobile phone to communicate by voice or text with another person while driving. So really all this prevented was texting and talking. If you think about it, most of the activities above do not include communicating with another "person" so that meant that they were all legal activities while driving.

GET DISMISSED: THE SEQUEL

Beginning in 2017, we now have a new hands-free law to live and drive by. The new law states the following:

- You cannot operate a motor vehicle while holding and operating a handheld wireless telephone or electronic wireless communication device unless;

- Your mobile phone is voice operated and in hands-free operation mode;

- Your phone must be mounted on your vehicle's windshield just like a GPS is, or affixed to the dashboard or center console that does not hinder the view of the road;

- Your phone can only be operated with a single swipe or tap of the finger

In other words, you can't type, you can't talk, you can't even hold your phone in your hand while doing nothing at all if you are operating a motor vehicle. By the way, this also applies anytime your motor is on even if you are stopped at a red light or parked.

I'm sure a lot of you enjoy listening to music on your mobile phones, I know I do. Here's another change to the law in 2017. Prior to 2017 you could listen to your music while driving with headphones or an ear piece, but you could only cover one ear; the other had to remain uncovered. Now, beginning in 2017, you cannot have any headphones or earpieces covering either ear if you are driving. I know, I know, how are you going to listen to your music while driving? How about using your Bluetooth or just use the speaker on the phone? But please remember, do not change the music unless your phone is mounted to your car.

Teenage drivers

- Currently teens are prohibited from all use of a mobile phone while driving during their first year of driving or until they are 18.

- Currently teens are prohibited from having other teens in the car with them while driving during their first year of driving or until they are 18.

- Traffic crashes are the leading cause of death for teens.

- Teens are the most likely to text and talk behind the wheel.

- More teens are involved in crashes from talking or attending to other passenger in the vehicle, than using a cell phone.

- New bill introduced could raise the age that new drivers must hold a provisional license from 18 to 21.

- Said to decrease accidents by raising age to 21

GET DISMISSED: THE SEQUEL

So maybe put your phone away next time you're driving and check out these interesting facts:

- 3,179 people were killed, and 431,000 were injured involving distracted driving in 2014

- 4,477 lives were claimed by distracted driving, and 391,00 people were injured in 2015

- 10% of all drivers ages 15-19, involved in fatal crashes, were from distracted driving

- Drivers in their 20s are 23% of drivers in all fatal crashes, but are 27% of distracted drivers and 38% of the distracted drivers who were using cell phones in fatal crashes

- 5 seconds is the average time your eyes are off the road while texting. When traveling at 55mph, that enough time to cover the length of a football field while you're essentially blindfolded

- At any giving moment over 660,000 drivers are operating cellphones or electronic devices while driving

And while you're at it, check out the United States Department of Transportations website for the national Highway Traffic Safety Administration, NHTSA, https://www.distraction.gov/stats-research-laws/facts-and-statistics.html.

GET DISMISSED: THE SEQUEL

Most Common Traffic Violations Codes and Descriptions

- Carpool:

- Crossing a Double Yellow:

  - Violation Code: 21655.8 (a)

  - Description: driving over double lines of preferential lanes

  - Carpool – Solo in HOV Lane:

    - Violation Code: 21655.5(b)

    - Description: improper use of preferential lanes

- Cell Phone:

  - Texting

    - Violation Code: 23123.5.

    - Description: improperly holding and using a cell phone while driving

  - Talking:

- Violation Code: 23123

- Description: improperly talking on a cell phone without a hands-free device while driving

- Failure to Yield:

  - Pedestrian

    - Violation Code: 21950

    - Description: failure to yield to a pedestrian at a marked or unmarked crosswalk

  - Moving Emergency vehicle

    - Violation Code: 21806

    - Description: failure to yield to an emergency vehicle that is exhibiting lights and sirens

  - Stopped Emergency vehicle

    - Violation Code: 21809

    - Description: failure to slow down or move over when approaching a stopped emergency vehicle on a freeway

- Another vehicle

  - Violation Code: 21800

  - Description: failure to yield to the right of way of another vehicle at an intersection

- No U-Turn:

  - Sign:

    - Violation Code: 21461(a)

    - Description: failure to obey a sign prohibiting making a U-turn

  - Business district:

    - Violation Code: 22102

    - Description: unlawfully making a U-turn in a business district

- Out of Lane:

  - Violation Code: 21658

  - Description: failure to stay in lane or lane straddling

- Passing Across Double Yellow Lines:

- Violation Code: 21460

- Description: improperly driving to the left of double yellow lines or crossing double yellow lines to pass other vehicles

- Red Light

  - Camera:

    - Violation Code: 21453

    - Description: failure to stop at a red light at an intersection equipped with a red light camera

  - Officer:

    - Violation Code: 21453

    - Description: disobeying a red signal at an intersection

  - Flashing Red Light:

    - Violation Code: 21457

    - Description: failure to stop at an intersection with a flashing red light

- Seatbelt:

- Violation Code: 27315

- Description: failure to properly wear a safety belt while driving or riding in a motor vehicle

- Sign Violation

  - Any sign

    - Violation Code: 21461

    - Description: failure to obey a posted sign or traffic control device

  - Stop sign

    - Violation Code: 22450

    - Description: failure to stop or improper stop at a stop sign

- Speeding

  - Over 100 MPH

    - Violation Code: 22348(b)

    - Description: exceeding 100 mph in any speed limit zone

GET DISMISSED: THE SEQUEL

- Over 70 MPH

  - Violation Code: 22356(b)

  - Description: exceeding 70 mph in a 70 mph speed limit zone

- Over 65 MPH

  - Violation Code: 22349(a)

  - Description: exceeding 65 mph in a 65 mph speed limit zone

- Over 55

  - Violation Code: 22349(b)

  - Description: exceeding 55 mph in a 55 mph speed limit zone

- Towing

  - Violation Code: 22406(b)

  - Description: exceeding 55 mph when towing in a passenger vehicle

- Unsafe speed

- Violation Code: 22350

- Description: driving at a speed that is unsafe for conditions in any speed limit zone

- Commercial Violations:

  - Log Book

    - Violation Code: 34501

    - Description: failure of a commercial driver to produce a completed log book upon demand by an officer

  - Out of Lane

    - Violation Codes: 22348(c); 21658

    - Description: failure to use lanes designated for commercial vehicles

  - Speeding

    - Violation Code: 22406(a)

    - Description: exceeding 55 mph when driving a commercial vehicle

  - Overweight

- Violation Code: 35551(a)

- Description: driving a vehicle that exceeds the legal weight limit for the number of axles and the distance between groups of axles

- Overlength

  - Violation Code: 35400

  - Description: driving a vehicle that exceed the legal length limit of 40 feet for semitrailers having two or more axles, or 38 feet for semis having one axle.

Basic Speeding

Basic Speed Rule
(Safe Speed) No person shall drive a vehicle at a speed greater than is reasonable or prudent having due regard for weather, visibility, the traffic on, and surface and width of, the highway.

Statutory (Maximum) Speed Limit
- 100 MPH – in addition to other speed laws can never exceed 100 MPH

- 65 MPH – most urban interstates, unless otherwise posted

- 70 MPH - many rural interstates, only if posted 70 MPH sign

- 55 MPH - trucks and autos towing and all vehicles on two lane undivided highways unless otherwise posted

Posted Prima Facie Speed Limit
Based on engineering and traffic surveys, a local government may decrease the statutory speed limits and establish prima facie speed limits of 60, 55, 50, 45, 40, 35, 30 or 25 MPH with posted signs.

Example: 25 MPH for business, residential, or school district

GET DISMISSED: THE SEQUEL

Minimum Speed Limit
A person shall not drive a vehicle at such a slow speed as to impede or block the normal and reasonable movement of traffic.

Penalties
· All Law Speed Violations are Infractions

· Above 100 MPH - $900+ and 2 points (CDL 2 ½)

· Speeding 1 -15 MPH over limit - $238+ and 1 point (CDL 1 ½)

· Speeding 16-25 MPH over limit - $367+ and 1 point (CDL 1 ½)

· Speeding 26 MPH or more over limit – 490+ and 1 point (CDL 1 ½)

· going too slow $238+ and 1 point

Traffic Ticket Tips

How to Avoid a Cell Phone Ticket
There's an app for everything these days. Some of which may even help to avoid a ticket. Like an app that can lock your smartphone while your car is in motion or an app that can monitor for distracted driving.

These apps may prove especially useful for parents of young drivers since teens cannot use a phone while driving (except for emergencies) whether it's hands-free or not.

How to Fight a Cell Phone Ticket
Are you a driver who tried using a speaker-phone far enough away from your head to make it look like your hands were free but still got a ticket? Police are very knowledgeable about all of these common "fake-it" techniques. Here are some tips for fighting that cell phone ticket you've got - just remember your ABC's:

Authorized purpose: It is not illegal to use a phone for emergency purposes or while on private property, so you can argue you were using your phone for an authorized purpose. Additionally, you can use you phone so long as its mounted and as long as you only use one finger to tap or swipe once.

Built in system: It is illegal to use a phone in a manner that is not hands free to communicate with another person and to hold a phone to use its applications. But these days many vehicles have a built-in system that allows you to control your phone and utilize its applications through your vehicle. Vehicle code 23123.5, the section that restricts operating a cell phone while driving, does not apply to manufacturer-installed systems that are embedded in your vehicle.

Cell Usage Records: It is your word against the officer's that you were not using the phone. Beef up your testimony of the events by showing the court a copy of your call log from your cell phone bill which shows no calls or texts were made or received at the time of the ticket.

How to Spot a Phony Red Light Camera Ticket
While red light camera use is on the decline there are many cities left throughout California where red light cameras are still active.

So if you received a red light camera ticket make sure it's not a scam.

There are tell-tale signs to look for like a due date and courthouse which a "phony" ticket will not have.

How to Fight a Red Light
Camera Ticket – Sign Posting
It is a requirement for red light camera intersections to be sign-posted warning drivers.

Proving otherwise can aid in the dismissal of a ticket:

• Take photos of the intersection.

• Measure the distance that signs are from the intersection (signs must be posted within 200 feet of the intersection)

How to Fight a Red Light
Camera Ticket – Signal Timing
The length of a yellow light or amber light can affect how many drivers are caught by red light cameras.

So, time the light, because if the yellow light is not legally long enough, it's a perfectly valid reason for a ticket to be dismissed.

The yellow light time must meet California's legal requirements - which varies from three to five-seconds depending on the posted speed limit.

How to Avoid Paying Double in a Construction Zone
Under California law the "construction zone fine" only applies during hours when work is actually being performed.

To avoid paying more when not required take photos of the area showing there are no "men at work."

You'll want to use a camera with a date/time stamp feature and for the date/time to be very close to that which is listed on your ticket.

GET DISMISSED: THE SEQUEL

Tip: Many smartphone cameras do not have a date/time stamp feature. There are apps available for your smartphone that will record the date, time, and even the location (e.g. iPhoto or Timestamp Camera).

How a Little Prep Time Can Help You Avoid a Ticket

In California it's unlawful to operate any vehicle in an unsafe condition presenting an immediate safety hazard. This could include driving with a flat or worn-out tire, broken signals or even dirty windows that obstruct your view.

While it may seem impractical to do this each time before you drive, a few seconds of prep time involving a quick "once around" vehicle inspection can save you from being stuck later: either on the side of the road or with a traffic ticket.

How to Avoid a Ticket for Unsafe Backing

A ticket for unsafe backing violation can add a point to your driving record.

Remember these simple safe backing tips:

- Do turn your body and look out of the rear window for any obstacles before driving in reverse;

- Don't closely watch your instrument panel while backing up; and

- Don't rely exclusively on your mirrors when in reverse

GET DISMISSED: THE SEQUEL

Four Techniques to Improve Your Driving in Foggy Weather

First and foremost slow down! You cannot see that far ahead of your vehicle in the fog and thus you have less reaction time to any potential hazards and changes in the roadway.

Fog is basically a collection of cold and heavy moisture in the air. As you drive through it the water will attach to your windshield. In order to increase your visibility use your wiper blades often to clear the windshield.

Switch on the defroster to reduce any condensation that the wiper blades cannot remove.

Lastly, turn on your low beams to further increase your visibility.

How to Avoid a Seatbelt Ticket

Wear your seatbelt properly and make it noticeable:

- Avoid wearing tops the same color as your seatbelt; if you are wearing your seatbelt the officer may not be able to tell.

- The lap belt is not enough since the law says the across the shoulder belt must be worn as well.

How to Avoid a Speeding Ticket

Don't make yourself a target for a speeding ticket:

- Avoid switching lanes unnecessarily;

- Avoid excessive passing;

- Avoid following too close (or tailgating);

- Watch for posted speed limit signs instead of going by the flow of traffic; and

- Avoid giving the officer extra incentive to stop you by having up-to-date tags and legal window tint

How to Fight a Speeding Ticket
To build your speeding defense it's key to narrow down the officer's position and the method used to "clock" your speed:

- Take note of where the officer was when you first saw him or her and if you were followed for a while or pulled over right away.

- The officer may mention the manner in which you were clocked such as that you were followed or that another officer clocked you during the traffic stop – take note of this.

- Check your ticket – Most tickets have a "radar" box which the officer uses to mark off a speed gun (radar or lidar) or to indicate that he followed you, (pacing method), or if a police airplane was used to clock your speed.

- If the officer just followed you (bumper pace) you should try to take note of how long the officer followed you or if he just came out of nowhere and caught up to you very quickly.

How to Avoid a Ticket for Failing to Stop for a School Bus

Never pass a stopped school bus with its red lights flashing and stop sign out.

If a school bus is stopped and you are on a two-lane road with no divider then you are required to stop whether you approach it from front or behind.

Keep an eye out for children at bus stops.

How to Avoid Getting Pulled Over

Avoid making yourself a target by avoiding these five "unwise" moves:

UN – Unsafe condition (like driving with bald tires);

W – Weaving in and out of lanes (draws more attention to your speed);

I – Improperly loaded vehicles (draws police attention to your vehicle);

S – Signal light out (gives police additional reason to stop you); and

E – Expired registration (again you are giving police extra incentive to stop you)

What to Do When You Are Being Pulled Over
You see the flashing lights behind you. Now what?

- Stay calm.

- Pull over immediately and in a safe manner.

- Do not stop on the left shoulder; even if you are in the carpool or fast lane (if in the carpool lane you must yield to the officer even if it means crossing over the double yellow lines).

- Use your turn signal when yielding.

- Pull over on the right shoulder and far enough over so the officer can stand safely.

How to Make a Traffic Stop Go Smoothly
- Remain seated in your vehicle with your seatbelt on and the engine off.

- Place your keys on the dash and keep both hands on the wheel.

- If it's dark then turn on your interior light to put the officer at ease.

- Ask permission before reaching for anything.

- Be polite and follow instructions.

- Do not admit to any wrongdoing; and the same goes for any passengers in the car with you.

- Doesn't hurt to ask for a warning but don't press the issue if the answer you get is "no."

You've Just Been Handed a Ticket. Now What?

- Sign it and refrain from threatening the officer with your intent to fight it.

- Don't say anything memorable or whip out your camera in front of the officer.

- Take a couple seconds to jot down a few notes about the traffic, driving conditions and anything the officer said to you during the stop.

- Pull back out onto the road safely using your signal.

- Return to the location as soon as you can and take photos of anything relevant to your ticket such as road signs or road conditions.

How to Prepare to Contest a Speeding Ticket

Take notes of anything that could have prevented the officer from clearly seeing what you did or didn't do;

GET DISMISSED: THE SEQUEL

Request relevant documents, referred to as "informal discovery." You can request documents like the officer's notes, training certificates, and maintenance and calibration logs for any speed measurement device used;

If you were cited for "unsafe speed" you can make a public records request to the city where you received the ticket for the speed survey on the street where you received the ticket. The speed survey may show the posted speed limit is too low. If the speed limit is set too low the officer is not allowed to use radar/lidar giving reason the ticket should be dismissed.

How to Prepare to Contest a Sign Violation
· Take photos of anything blocking the sign;

· Document anything that could have prevented you from seeing the sign like a tall, parked vehicle for example.

How to Prepare to Contest Other Types of Tickets
· Make a diagram showing your location, the officer's location, and any obstructions that were between you like other vehicles for example;

· Gather statements from any witnesses and if you had a passenger get a written account of what happened from them and get it notarized.

Your New Driver License – The REAL ID

The time has come for all Californians to finally upgrade their driver's license to a REAL ID driver license. We're not talking about your typical new driver's license that most of you receive in the mail when it's time to renew, but instead you have the opportunity to be issued a completely new ID card that was mandated as part of REAL ID Act of 2005 and passed in response to 9/11 that created new security standards for states driver licenses and IDs.

This is the biggest change to ID cards and driver licenses in years, yet most people haven't heard about it, let alone know when they need to upgrade or even how to get their new REAL ID card. The government and the DMV have done little to inform the public and there has been very little media coverage. Not to worry, we're here to change that, so let's begin.

What is the REAL ID and why do I need it?
The REAL ID is a federally compliant driver's license or ID card that all travelers will need if you plan to travel within the United States after October 1, 2020. The U.S. Department of State, states that "Effective January 22, 2018 air travelers with identification (ID) that does not meet the REAL ID Act requirements or whose State does not have an extension must present an alternative form of ID in order to board a domestic flight." Basically, if you plan to travel domestically beginning in 2018, you may want to consider upgrading your

driver's license to the new REAL ID. Without a REAL ID, it may also be a smart move to bring your passport when you're traveling in order to avoid any potential issues with TSA and all their security checkpoints. We know you wouldn't want to miss your flight, so why not be prepared.

Previously there were nine states whose ID cards to not comply with the federal minimum-security requirements including, Kentucky, Main, Minnesota, Missouri, Montana, Oklahoma, Pennsylvania, South Carolina, and Washington. However, all these states have subsequently receive federal extensions to become compliant. All other states currently comply with the REAL ID, including California, so you can continue to use your state-issued driver's license or ID to fly in the U.S. until October 1, 2020, but we suggest you upgrade to the REAL ID as soon as possible.

Keep in mind that you do not need a new REAL ID to drive, vote, or if you do not plan on flying domestically.

When do I need to upgrade my driver's license to the new REAL ID?

Beginning January 22, 2018, all California DMV offices will begin accepting applications for the new REAL ID driver's license and identification cards required by the Federal REAL ID Act. As a result, all California drivers who would like the new REAL ID, will be required to visit the DMV to upgrade their driver's license to the new REAL ID driver's license if they plan to travel domestically. Remember, you have up and until October 1, 2020 to get your new ID card, however it pays to get it sooner rather than later, especially if you plan on traveling.

How do I upgrade my driver license to the REAL ID?
You cannot apply for a REAL ID by mail, you must apply in person at your local DMV office. When applying for your new ID card, you must bring physical copies of more documents than currently required for a regular California driver license. These documents include:

• Proof of identity, such as a U.S. birth certificate or passport;

• Proof of California residency – this can be a rental or lease agreement, home utility bill, mortgage bill or another approved document;

• Proof of social security number such as your social security card or a paycheck that discloses your social security number; and

• If you change your name, got married or divorced, you may need to prove additional documents. You should be prepared to show a marriage license, dissolution of marriage/domestic partnership, or name change documents to establish your true full name.

• You can find a list of all approved documents here - https://www.dmv.ca.gov/portal/wcm/connect/2db22455-e270-47a3-819c-d7c7716d5194/List_of_Docs_REALID.pdf?MOD=AJPERES

GET DISMISSED: THE SEQUEL

It's always best to make an appointment at the DMV if you plan to upgrade your driver license as we expect the all DMV offices to be extremely busy during this time.

We believe that the changing over to the new REAL ID is a smart move. This will standardize the ID requirement across all states that currently have various ID standards and make your identification more secure and safe. We are advising all Californians to make an appointment with your local DMV office and upgrade to the new REAL ID. You may also want to make sure your passport is current or order a passport if you don't have one just to be safe.

Traffic Ticket Myths

There are a lot of misconceptions out there when it comes to traffic laws and tickets so let's get it straight.

It's better for you if you don't sign on the dotted line (of a traffic ticket). MYTH!
Without your signature on the citation the officer would have to arrest you and nobody wants that.

Your signature allows the police officer to release you from the traffic stop. Think of it as your "promise" to take care of the ticket on or before the due date.

In California you can't drive barefoot. MYTH!
Despite there being no California law that prevents you from driving barefoot, many people assume it is illegal.

This has most likely become a popular myth do to the safety factors that come to mind: bare feet can sweat and make you lose traction on the pedal. A shoe's sole gives you a sturdy contact surface making for easy placement on those pedals.

When driving in the carpool lane the solid white line on the inside of the double yellow line means you can cross it. MYTH!
There are many uses for a single solid white line. Generally, it's used when crossing the line is discouraged.

A double yellow line on the other hand is used not merely to discourage crossing, but to prohibit it. A double yellow trumps the solid white line so crossing is not only discouraged, it's prohibited.

Police aren't allowed to record a traffic stop. MYTH!
If you get a ticket from a CHP officer and see "MVARS" marked on your ticket this means there was a dash cam recording the events that led to your stop. The recording usually begins as soon as the lights are activated.

Can they do this? Yes. But you can also ask for a copy of it. Score!

The Legal BAC to drive is the same no matter what type of vehicle you drive. MYTH!
Existing law forbids a person who has a BAC of 0.08% or more from driving a vehicle. But if you plan to drive a "commercial" vehicle (i.e. big rigs, school buses, vehicles carrying hazardous materials, and public transportation vehicles) you can't have a BAC any higher than 0.04%.

In California, if you have a commercial driver license you can't take traffic school. MYTH!
Starting in 2011 you can take traffic school even if you have a commercial license.

What's the catch? You must have received the ticket while driving a non-commercial vehicle, like your normal car.

GET DISMISSED: THE SEQUEL

What's the other catch? A regular non-commercial driver can take traffic school to hide the fact they got a ticket. This means employers and insurance companies will not know about the ticket. For a commercial driver, even though you can take traffic school to remove the point, your employer and insurance company will be able to see you got a ticket.

You have to obey stop signs in a car but not on a bike. MYTH!
Stop signs are not optional for bicyclists, the same law applies.

A bicyclist who fails to stop for a stop sign can be ticketed just like the driver of a car and under the same law too - Vehicle Code section 22450.

When you get a ticket as a pedestrian or a bicyclist a point could go on your driver record just like if you were driving a car. MYTH!
Any violation occurring as a pedestrian or a bicyclist has no point assigned.

According to the California DMV, violation points are only assigned to Vehicle Code sections (and any other code section, or city or county ordinance) involving the safe operation of a motor vehicle.

To drive in California, you must have a California license. MYTH!
You generally will not be required to get a California license according to the vehicle code if you:

- are over 18;

- you live in another state; and

- have a valid driver license issued by your home state.

When driving with a pet the pet can be loose. MYTH!
In California you can't drive with any animal in the back of the vehicle (like the bed of a truck), unless the animal is secured in such a manner as to prevent jumping or falling from the vehicle.

Lane-splitting is illegal in California. MYTH!
Lane-splitting by a motorcyclist remains legal if done safely.

It's illegal to text while driving but it's ok to use Facebook. MYTH!
In California it is illegal to manually type or read messages. This is commonly thought to mean only texting while driving is prohibited. But there are other ways to "manually communicate" like instant messaging or even...posting on Facebook.

You have to let police officers search your phone during a traffic stop if they suspect you've been texting while driving. MYTH!
Police can't search your phone without your permission or a search warrant. They can ask but you don't have to let them.

GET DISMISSED: THE SEQUEL

When towing or driving a commercial truck you can only drive in the far right lane. MYTH!
Absent a sign stating otherwise, commercial vehicles and vehicles towing trailers can be driven in either of the far right two lanes on a highway having four or more lanes (California Vehicle Code 22348 (c).

In California it's illegal for police to park out of view (in hiding) when enforcing the speed limit. MYTH!
There is no law in California that says police have to be parked in plain view when measuring the speed of passing cars.

Just like red light camera tickets you can get a speeding ticket in the same way, through the mail. MYTH!
Although the State of California has permitted use of red light camera enforcement for some time now the state does not yet allow for speed camera enforcement.

Radar detectors are illegal in California. MYTH!
Unlike jammers which seek to interfere with radar used by police to measure the speed of moving objects, radar detectors are legal in most places in California so long as it is not mounted on the windshield where it could obstruct the driver's vision.

If you get in an accident regardless of how minor, you must report it to the DMV. MYTH!
If you hit someone or someone hits you and nobody got hurt then swapping information is usually enough. If you are

involved in a vehicle accident that occurred in California, you must report it to DMV in 10 days only if:

- there was property damage (over $1,000); or

- people are injured (even minor injuries) or there are fatalities.

You are required to talk to the officer during the traffic stop. MYTH!
During a traffic stop it's best to be cooperative but also remember your right to remain silent. You are not obligated to admit to any wrongdoing.

If you ask to see the radar gun the officer must show it you. MYTH!
While many officers are more than happy to accommodate your request there is no law in California saying they have to - and for safety or policy reasons they may not be able to.

Traffic Ticket Glossary of Terms

Get familiar with terms you will come across when contesting your traffic ticket.

Abstract
A summary of what a court or government agency does.

Acknowledgment
Saying, testifying, or assuring that something is true. You can say this out loud or write it down.

Acquittal
When a judge or jury finds that the person on trial is not guilty.

Admissible evidence
Evidence that can legally and properly be used in court.

Admission
Saying that certain facts are true. But not saying you are guilty.

Affidavit
 A written statement that someone swears to under oath in front of someone that is legally authorized, like a judge or notary public.

Allegation
A statement or claim that is made and hasn't been proved to be true or false.

Allege
To say, declare, or charge that something is true even though it isn't proved yet.

Appeal
When someone that loses at least part of a case and requests a higher court perform a review of a lower court ruling.

Appearance
Going to court. Or, a legal paper that says you will participate in the court process.

Arraignment
Bringing a defendant before a judicial officer to allow him or her to hear the charges that were filed and make a plea.

Bail
A security deposit, usually money, given to release a defendant or witness from custody and to ensure that they go to court appearances when they're supposed to.

Bail forfeiture
A court order to let the court keep the bail deposit because the defendant didn't go to court when they were supposed to.

GET DISMISSED: THE SEQUEL

Bailiff
A person assigned by a sheriff or marshal to provide security to the court.

Burden of proof
When one person in the case has the responsibility to give more evidence than the other person.

Calendar
A categorized list of cases to be heard in a court at specific dates and times; to assign a date, time, and court to a case.

California Rules of Court
The rules for practices and procedures in California's state courts.

Case
A legal dispute brought to a court for resolution.

Caseload
The number of cases a judge has in a specific time.

Case number
The number automatically assigned to a case by the court - sometimes different from the citation number.

Change of venue
When a civil or criminal case is moved from one court jurisdiction to another.

Charge
In criminal law, the formal statement of each accusation against a defendant.

Citation
A ticket issued by an officer for violating a traffic statute.

Citation number
A number which is printed on the ticket issued by an officer for violating a traffic statute. You will need to reference this number in your dealings with the court.

Citing authority or agency
An agency related to the court, like the city police or the California Highway Patrol, that can arrest people for breaking the law and issue traffic tickets.

Civil collections
When the Court issues a civil judgment against your case the outstanding fine can be pursued civilly by the County's Collection Agency. This civil judgment may be collected the same way as any other civil judgment: by attachment of your wages, bank accounts, other property, or by tax intercept of any tax refunds. The civil judgment will remain in effect for 10 years or until paid.

Clerk of court
A person chosen by the judges to help manage cases, keep court records, deal with financial matters, and give other administrative support.

GET DISMISSED: THE SEQUEL

Clocked
Refers to how the officer measured your speed, which can be one of several methods:

- **Radar** – A type of electronic speed measuring device that uses radar waves to measure speed. Can be used in moving mode (like when an officer is driving in the opposite direction of you). Officer needs clear line of sight. Serial Numbers usually start with "DC," "AT," "AS," or just a set of numbers with no letters.

- **Laser/Lidar** – Laser and Lidar are terms used interchangeably. It is a type of electronic speed measurement device that uses a beam of light to measure speed. Officer looks through scope on laser to view vehicle, places red dot on vehicle within scope then pulls trigger. Laser sends out beam of light and records approximately 13 speed readings within one second. Officer needs a clear line of sight to do this. Serial Numbers usually start with "T/S" or "U/X." Officer may also write "L" and circle it under description. There are no moving laser units.

- **Pace** – When officer is following from behind. Generally officer will write from "point A" to "point B." Or patrol vehicle number will be circled and there will be a line through radar/lidar.

- **Visual** – Generally nothing is checked off and no serial numbers are written on ticket. Ex: ticket will just say the location where your speed was seen by the officer like "s/b Hacienda/Los Altos."

- **Aircraft** – There is an officer in the plane that clocks the vehicle from the air. The air officer radios a ground officer to pull over the car. Generally, will have "plane" written on ticket in space for radar.

Codes
The law created by statutes. For example, the California Code of Civil Procedure, California Civil Code, California Vehicle Code, California Penal Code, and California Health and Safety Code.

Commissioner
A person appointed by the court that is given the power to hear and make decisions concerning certain legal matters.

Contempt of Court
An act or omission that obstructs the orderly administration of justice or impairs the dignity respect, or authority of the court.

Contested
A case in which evidence is introduced by both parties.

Continuance
A request to postpone a court date.

Conviction
The determination of guilt based on a plea, jury, verdict, or a finding of a judicial officer.

Count
One of what may be numerous charges filed, each for alleged violation of a separate offense.

Court
A judge or body of judges whose task it is to hear cases and administer justice.

Court costs
The money needed to pay for the operation of the court system.

Court order
A legal decision made by a court that commands or directs that something be done or not done. Can be made by a judge, commissioner, court referee, or magistrate.

Court trial
A trial in which there is no jury and in which a judicial officer determines both the issues of fact and the law in a case.

Courtesy notice
A notice made by a computer that is usually sent for traffic violations to tell a defendant about a court date, bail, etc.

Decision
A judgment or decree that settles a legal issue.

GET DISMISSED: THE SEQUEL

Declaration
A formal document, not necessarily made under oath, setting forth the facts that support's a party's legal allegations. Can be written or oral.

Defendant
A person required to answer a criminal accusation or civil complaint (the ticketed driver is a defendant when contesting the ticket).

Defense
A denial, answer, or plea disputing the correctness of the charges against a defendant.

De novo
Starting a case all over again as if it had not been heard before. In Latin, novo means "new."

Dismissal
The offense, or ticket, you have been charged with violating, has been dropped, so it will not affect your record.

Disposition
The final decision by the court in a dispute.

Docket
The permanent, cumulative record of all proceedings of a case; a list of cases on a court's calendar.

Evidence
Documents, testimony of parties or witnesses, or physical objects presented as proof during trial.

Exhibit
A document or an object shown and identified in court as evidence in a case.

Exonerate
To clear from blame, or to relieve of responsibility.

Failure to Appear (aka FTA)
When you fail to appear as promised on the citation you signed, the court will file a complaint charging you with Failure to Appear, under section 40508A of the California Vehicle Code, and will also impose a civil assessment under section 1214.1 of the Penal Code. In addition, The Department of Motor Vehicles will be notified to withhold renewal of your driver license and your driving privilege may be suspended. You may also be tried in absentia and a civil judgment entered against you.

Failure to Pay Fine (aka FTP)
When you fail to pay a fine imposed by the Court, your case becomes a failure to pay and a DMV HOLD is placed on your driver license.

Fix-it-Ticket (aka correctable violation)
Term for a traffic citation issued due to a mechanical malfunction on a vehicle.

GET DISMISSED: THE SEQUEL

Forfeiture
When a person must give up money or property because they didn't meet a legal obligation.

Guilty
Found beyond a reasonable doubt to have committed a crime.

Guilty plea
When a person admits in court that he or she is guilty of the crime charged in a criminal complaint, information, or indictment.

Hearing
A constitutionally required formal proceeding where the accused is given notice of charges brought against him or her and where the accused has an opportunity to present a defense.

Infraction
A minor violation of a law, contract, or right that is not a misdemeanor or a felony and that cannot be punished by imprisonment.

In limine
Latin for "at the beginning" or "at the threshold," such as a motion in limine at the beginning of trial to ask that certain evidence be excluded.

Innocent
Found by a court to be not guilty of criminal charges; acquitted.

GET DISMISSED: THE SEQUEL

Judge
An elected or appointed individual empowered by law to hear and determine disposition of legal issue.

Judgment
The official decision of a court that resolves a case.

Judicial officer
Judges, referees, and commissioners that make court decisions as a judge.

License hold
The action taken to prevent someone from renewing their driver's license until a legal matter is settled.

Misdemeanor
A crime or serious traffic violation that can be punished by up to one year in jail.

Motion
An oral or written request made by a party to the court for a ruling or an order on a party's point.

Notice
A written announcement or warning.

Offense
An act that violates the law.

GET DISMISSED: THE SEQUEL

Opinion
A judge's written explanation of the decision of the court in an appellate case.

Order
Decision of a judicial officer.

Pending
The status of a case that is not yet resolved by the court.

Perjury
A false statement made on purpose while under oath in a court proceeding.

Plea
A formal statement of a defendant in response to a criminal accusation. You can plead guilty (admit you did it), no contest (accept the penalty of committing the offense without admitted any wrongdoing), or not guilty (do not admit you did it).

Public record
A court record available for inspection by the general public.

Pro per or Pro se
Persons that present their own cases in court without lawyers.

Record
A written account of the proceedings in a case

GET DISMISSED: THE SEQUEL

Referee
A person appointed by the court to hear and make decisions on certain limited legal matters.

Registered owner
A "registered owner" is a person registered by the department as the owner of a vehicle.

Sentence
The formal pronouncement by a court stating the punishment to be imposed on a person convicted of a criminal offense.

Superior court
The trial court in each county of the State of California. This court hears traffic cases.

Testify
To give evidence under oath.

Traffic
The term "traffic" includes pedestrians, ridden animals, vehicles, streetcars, and other conveyances, either singly or together, while using any highway for purposes of travel.

Traffic offense
An act or omission, which relates to the regulation of traffic on the roads, highways or streets or the operation of self-propelled or non-self- propelled vehicles of any kind and for

which, upon conviction, imprisonment or fine, or both imprisonment and fine, is authorized.

Traffic Violator School
A "traffic violator school" is a business that, for compensation provides, or offers to provide, instruction in traffic safety, including, but not limited to, classroom.

Trial
a court proceeding where you plead your case (prove you are not guilty of what you have been accused of doing). Trials can be in writing or in person.

Tried in Absentia
The court will hold a trial without you being present.

Uphold
When an appellate court agrees with the lower court decision and allows it to stand.

Venue
The particular court in which an action may be brought.

Verdict
The final decision about the guilt or innocence of a criminal defendant made by a judge or jury.

Warrant
A written order issued and signed by a judicial officer directing a peace officer to take specific action.

Witness

A person who has knowledge of facts having to do with a case being tried and who gives testimony. In traffic court, the only witnesses are typically the police officer and the ticketed individual.

GET DISMISSED: THE SEQUEL

Conclusion

Have you had enough of us by now? We've had enough, so we will just stop right here and get to the end.

You now know what we know and we both know we can fight that traffic ticket. Don't be afraid! We feel that just about any ticket can be contested and has a possibility of being dismissed if you just follow our methodology properly.

You see, in California, traffic ticket revenue is the number two revenue generator in the entire state. So, the government will continue to look for creative ways to issue more tickets and raise revenue for the State of California. In reality, traffic tickets are just another way to tax individuals.

As we've presented throughout this book you do have options and you can use these options to your advantage. What if we told you that there's a better way than just paying your traffic ticket? A way that, if successful, would save you money so that no point goes on your driving record, your insurance doesn't go up, and your traffic fine is refunded to you. And in the worst case if unsuccessful you are right back where you started. You could contest your case in court and get another bite at the apple (second chance to get back at the "man") or just request traffic school or pay the fine. You would say: "Ya! Let's do this!" By now you know that we're talking about a Trial by Written Declaration.

So, GetDismissed huh? An app that facilitates this process? Yes, were talking about the GetDismissed Mobile and Web app. This is really a no brainer. You got the traffic ticket and if you do nothing else, at the very least you'll need to pay the traffic ticket. So why not take a chance to keep it off your record and get your money back? Download the GetDismissed app, take pictures of your traffic ticket and driver license, pay the nominal fee, and get access to all the completed documents you need to print and file with the court to contest your traffic ticket. It's that simple.

There's an acronym used in business, marketing, software development and many other places called KISS: KEEP IT SIMPLE STUPID!

We believe this makes sense when discussing traffic tickets. Don't over think it, just KISS and your traffic ticket will GetDismissed!

Download the GetDismissed app for free at www.GetDismissed.com or at the Apple iTunes or Google Play stores.